NOTES

ON

PHILIPPIANS

By H. A. IRONSIDE

Author of "Holiness: The False and the True;"
"Praying in the Holy Spirit;" "Death and Afterwards;"
"Letters to a Roman Catholic Priest," etc.

NEW EDITION—REVISED

LOIZEAUX BROTHERS, PUBLISHERS,
19 WEST 21st STREET
NEW YORK

BIBLE TRUTH PRESS
19 W. 21st ST., N. Y.

———

**Printed in the United States
of America**

PREFATORY NOTE

THESE *notes have been jotted down at odd times, over a period of nearly two years, while the writer has been busily engaged in gospel work. They pretend to no literary value, and repetitions may sometimes occur, but such as they are, they are sent forth with the earnest hope that they may be blessed to some of "the quiet in the land" who enjoy simple things, plainly put.*

H. A. IRONSIDE.

July, 1922.

CONTENTS

———

Contents

CHAPTER THREE

Christ the Believer's Object, and the Steadfast Mind

CHAPTER FOUR

Christ, the Believer's Strength, and the Confident Mind

NOTES ON
PHILIPPIANS

Introductory Thoughts

THE account of the labors and sufferings of the apostle Paul and his companions, in Philippi, is given in the 16th chapter of the Acts. They went to Macedonia in response to the vision of the man of that country calling for help, which Paul had seen at Troas. But when they reached the capital, there was apparently no such man feeling his need and awaiting them. Instead, they came first in touch with a few women who were accustomed to gather for prayer n a quiet place, by the riverside, outside the city. There the Lord opened Lydia's heart to attend to the things spoken by Paul. Others too were evidently reached; among them some brethren, as verse 40 makes clear. But it was when cast into prison that the greatest work was done. The jailer and his household were won for Christ ere the messengers of God's grace took their departure for Thessalonica.

The infant church was very dear to the heart of the apostle, and he was very dear to them. Their love and care were shown after he left them, at various times, and, one would judge, for a number of years. But at last they lost touch with him, apparently during his imprisonment at Cæsarea. It was when he was in Rome that they again got into communication with him and fearing he might be in need, sent him an expression of their love and care by the hand of a trusted and beloved brother who was one of themselves, Epaphroditus. Having fulfilled his ministry, this faithful man fell sick, and his illness was of sufficient duration for word regarding it to reach Philippi, and the news of the anxiety of the saints there concerning him had come back to Rome about the time that he became convalescent. Deciding at once to return, he was entrusted with the letter we have before us, which was, one would judge, dictated to him by the apostle.

It is an epistle of joy, a letter of cheer. On the

other hand, it contains needful exhortation for a wilderness people, liable to fall out by the way.

It would seem that Epaphroditus had communicated to Paul a certain concern that was weighing upon his heart regarding a misunderstanding or a positive quarrel between two women in the assembly—both much esteemed by the saints and by the apostle himself—which if not checked and healed, was likely to prove a source of sadness, and possibly even division in days to come.

This appears to be much in the apostle's mind as he indites his epistle. He seeks so to present Christ that the hearts of all may be ravished with Him, and thus all selfish aims disappear, and all that is of the flesh be judged in His presence.

This is ever what is needed when the flesh is at work among believers. Therefore the great importance of this portion of the Word of God in the present hour of the Church's history.

The epistle falls very naturally into four divisions, and these are rightly indicated in our common version by the four chapters. The theme of the whole might be put in the three words, *"Christ is all!"* It is the epistle of Christ. It occupies us with Himself; and each separate division presents Him in some different way, and indicates the subjective result in the believer as he is occupied with Christ objectively in the manner presented.

Chapter one sets forth Christ as our Life, and the evangelistic spirit or the gospel mind.

In chapter two we have Christ as our Example, and the lowly mind, or the humble spirit of those who would follow Him.

Chapter three gives us Christ as our Object, and, subjectively, we have the steadfast spirit, the determined mind; that is, the heart and thoughts centered on Himself.

In the last chapter Christ is set forth as our Strength and Supply, and naturally we have with this the confident mind, the spirit of trust that should characterize all who know the resources that are in Him.

It will be readily seen that the epistle is a very practical one. It has to do with our state rather than our standing ; with responsibility rather than privilege; with communion rather than with union. In other words, it is an epistle suited to our wilderness journey. It was written to guide our feet while going through this world. It is a pastoral ministry of a very precious kind.

Others have written very fully and helpfully on this part of the Word of God, whose writings are readily obtainable. It is not the present writer's thought to attempt a labored exposition of the epistle, but simply to jot down some notes which embody the results of his own study, and which it is hoped may be used by the Holy Spirit for the edification and comfort of fellow-saints, particularly such as are becoming discouraged because of the way. Much has been gleaned from what others have set forth, and no pretension is made as to originality of treatment. If Christ Himself becomes a little more appreciated by a few of His own, the object in view will have been attained.

CHAPTER ONE

CHRIST, THE BELIEVER'S LIFE, AND THE EVANGELISTIC SPIRIT

Salutation

(vers. 1, 2.)

"Paul and Timothy, servants of Jesus Christ, to all the saints in Christ Jesus who are at Philippi, with the bishops and deacons; Grace to you and peace, from God our Father and the Lord Jesus Christ."

IT is noticeable how, in many of his letters, the apostle links up younger and less experienced fellow-laborers with himself, as here, in his salutations. He was an apostle by the Lord's call, occupying a unique place as His special messenger to the Gentiles. But he never stands aloof in complacent dignity apart from others who are engaged in the same ministry. He had taken Timothy with him when the latter had not long been in the knowledge and path of the truth, and he testifies later, in this same letter, of the truth that was in him. In his care for the development of the younger brethren, Paul becomes a model for older teachers and evangelists to the end of the dispensation. If others are to follow on in the ways that be in Christ, it is well that more experienced men take a personal interest in their less experienced brethren who manifest a measure of gift, and by associating them with themselves in ministry, lead and encourage them in the path of faith. It is often the other way, and the young are disheartened, and permitted to slip back into business pursuits, who, if wisely advised, and helped when needed, might become able ministers of the truth.

Paul and Timothy take no official title here. They are simply servants of Jesus Christ. The word means *bondmen*. They were purchased servants, and as such, belonged entirely to Him whom they gladly owned as their Anointed Master. They were His by right, and they had renounced all title to do the will of the flesh. Nor is it only ministering brethren who are so designated in Scripture. This is the name that is used of all Christians. Though sons and heirs we are also bondmen of love, whose delight it should be to yield ourselves unto Him as those that are alive from the dead.

The saints as a whole at Philippi are greeted, and the elders and deacons specially mentioned. This is unusual. It evidently implies a particular sense of obligation to the elders and deacons on

the part of the apostle, probably in connection
with ministry of the assembly's gift of love. There
may also be the thought of addressing the leaders,
or guides, in a special way, in view of the "rift
in the lute"—the unhappiness between Euodia
and Syntyche, which he desired to rectify.

Elders may, or may not, be official. In the
early church they were definitely appointed by
apostolic authority. It may be unwise, and going
beyond Scripture, for saints in feebleness to-day
to set up or ordain official elders. On the other
hand, those measurably possessing the qualifica-
tions indicated in the epistles to Timothy and
Titus, should be recognized by fellow-believers as
God-appointed elders, whose counsel should be
sought, and who are responsible to watch for
souls and to take oversight in the house of God.
To fail to own such would be insubjection to the
Word of God, but a true bishop or overseer would
be the last man to insist upon obedience to him.
He would rather lead by serving the saints and
by the force of a godly example.

Deacons are those who minister in temporal
things, and should be chosen by the saints for this
purpose. The word means *servant,* but is different to that used above. It is not "bondman," but
a servant acting voluntarily, and in response
generally to the expressed desire of others.

Notice the little word "ALL." It is used very significantly in this epistle—in a way not found anywhere else in the writings of the apostle Paul.

Observe its use in verses 4, 7, 8, 25 in this chapter, and verse 26 in chapter 2. Is it not plain that Paul desired to bind all together in one bundle of love in this way, refusing to even seem to recognize any incipient division among them? He greeted them *all*, he thought well of them all, *he* prayed for them *all*. He knew it would in the end be well with them *all*. And so he exhorted them *all* to stand fast in one spirit.

As customary in all his letters, he wished them grace and peace. Grace was the general Grecian salutation. Peace was that of the Hebrew. So he links the two together. Grace in its highest sense, favor against desert, could only be known by the Christian. And true peace rests upon the work of the Cross, whether it be that peace *with* God, which is fundamental, or the peace *of* God, which the apostle here would have the saints enter into and enjoy from day to day. Both descend from God, now revealed as Father, and from our Lord Jesus Christ, through whom we have been brought into this place of favor.

The Introduction

(verses 3-11.)

"I thank my God upon every remembrance of you, always in every prayer of mine for you all, making request with joy, for your fellowship in the gospel from the first day until now; being confident of this very thing, that He which hath begun a good work in you will perform it until the day of Jesus Christ: even as it is meet for me to think this of you all, because I have you in my heart; inasmuch as both in my bonds, and in the defence and confirmation of the gospel, ye all are partakers of my grace. For God is my record, how greatly I long after you all in the bowels (or, tenderness) of Jesus Christ. And this I pray, that your love may abound yet more and more in knowledge and in all judgment (or, perception); that ye may approve things that are excellent; that ye may be sincere and without offence (or, blameless) till the day of Christ; being filled with the fruits of righteousness, which are by Jesus Christ, unto the glory and praise of God."

IN these verses we have the apostle's own introduction to this delightful specimen of early Christian correspondence. His interest in the saints at Philippi did not cease with his leaving their city. Through all the years that had passed he had borne them on his heart, and presented them to God in prayer. There were sweet and blessed memories too that filled him with gladness as he looked back on the season of ministry spent amongst them, and as he learned of their continuance in the grace of God in after days.

He thanks God upon every remembrance of them. There was nothing, apparently, in their past history that had caused him pain or anxiety of mind. And so, in every prayer of his for them all, he preferred his request with joy. Their fellowship with him in the gospel had been consistent from the beginning. It will be noticed what a large place "fellowship" has in this epistle, and also how frequently "the gospel" is mentioned. An assembly of saints walking together in the fear of the Lord, exercised about holding forth the Word of Life to the unsaved, is likely to know more of real fellowship than a company of believers occupied chiefly with their own affairs, their own blessings—all about *themselves*. On the other hand, no assembly can prosper that fails to recognize the importance of the divine and holy principles given in the Word to guide believers in this scene.

Fellowship in the gospel may be exercised in various ways: by prayer, by participation in the public testimony, by furnishing the means to enable the laborer to go forth unhindered by perplexities and anxieties as to necessary means to carry on his work. Every servant of Christ going forth for the Name's sake, "taking nothing of the Gentiles," should be entirely cast upon the Lord for his support. On the other hand, it should be esteemed a privilege on the part of those abiding at home, to help them by ministering in temporal things; and such ministry will never be forgotten by Him who has said, "Whosoever receiveth a prophet in the name of a prophet shall receive a prophet's reward."

I remember a brother's definition of fellowship. He was a teamster, and was asked, "What do you understand by fellowship?" He replied, "For each one to pull his own trace and keep it tight." The simile is a crude one, but will be readily understood.

It is noticeable that the apostle had no doubt as to the final outcome for every true believer. He was absolutely confident that the One who had begun a good work in them, would never leave off until He had perfected that which He Himself had commenced. But this would only be attained and manifested in the day of Jesus Christ. A godly old brother used often to say, "The Lord always looks at His people as they will be when they are done." And it is well for us if we can learn to look at them in the same way. An incident is told of an artist who had conceived in his mind a great picture, which he meant to be the masterpiece of his life. He was working on a large canvas, putting in the drabs and grays that were to compose the background, when a friend entered, unnoticed.

The artist worked on with enthusiasm, not aware of the onlooker's presence. But, finally happening to turn, he saw him, and exclaimed, "What do you think of this? I intend it to be the greatest work I have ever done." His friend burst into a laugh, and exclaimed, "Why, to be frank, I don't think much of it. It seems to me to be only a great daub." "Ah," replied the artist, at once sensing the situation, "you cannot see what is going to be there. I can." And so it is with God our Father. He sees in every believer that which will be fully brought out at the judgment-seat of Christ, and He is working now toward that end. We too often see the present imperfection and forget the future glory. But, in the day of Jesus Christ, when all shall be manifested, every believer will be conformed to the image of God's blessed Son. Surely we can join with the apostle even now and say, "It is meet for me to think this of you all." Thus to look upon God's people will deliver from much strife, and from disappointment, when we see crudities and carnalities in those from whom we had expected better things. It is humbling and healthful too to remember that others probably see similar imperfections in us.

Paul carried the saints in his heart, and, though himself in prison, he recognized their fellowship in the defence and confirmation of the gospel, and rejoiced in the manner in which they shared this grace with him. He calls God to witness how greatly he yearned after every one of them in the tender love of Christ Jesus; and in verses 9-11 we have his prayer, which reminds us somewhat of the prayer in Colossians 1. He would have their love abound yet more and more in knowledge and all perception, or discernment. Brotherly love is not a matter of mere sentimentality; it is love in the truth. And this calls for study of the Word of God in order that one may know just how to manifest that love according to each particular occasion. Let us remember there is never a time when we are not called upon to show love to our brother, but we cannot always manifest it in the same way, if subject to the Word of God. Therefore the need of instruction in that Word, and enlightenment by the Holy Spirit, that we may perceive what is in accordance with the mind of God.

The first clause in the 10th verse is sometimes rendered, "That ye may try the things that differ;" or, as given above, "Approve things that are excellent." The meaning is practically the same. For by testing things that differ, we approve what is excellent. Again the test is the Word of God. That Word is given to try all things, and it will manifest what is truly excellent, thus giving the believer to understand how he may walk so as to please God, that he may be sincere and blameless in the day of Christ.

Attention has often been called to the striking fact that we have here the Anglicized Latin word "sincere," meaning, literally, "without wax"—used to translate a Greek word meaning "sun-tested." It might seem at first as though there is no connection between the two terms. But we are told that the ancients had a very fine porcelain which was greatly valued, and brought a very high price. This ware was so fragile, that it was only with the greatest difficulty it could be fired without being cracked; and dishonest dealers were in the habit of filling in the cracks that appeared with a pearly-white wax, which looked enough like the true porcelain to pass without being readily detected in the shops. If held to the light, however, the wax was at once manifested as a dark seam; and honest Latin dealers marked their wares "sine cera" (without wax). Thus the apostle would have the saints tested by the sunlight of God's truth and holiness, and found to be without wax; that is, he would have them straightforward, and honorable in all their dealings. Anything that savors of sham or hypocrisy is as the wax used to hide the imperfection in the porcelain.

"Blameless" (see also ver. 15 of chap. 2) refers to *motive* rather than to act, I take it. It is not the same thing as "sinless," which would, of course, imply complete moral perfection. "Blamelessness" implies right motives. "The fruits of righteousness" of verse 11 is the same as in Hebrews 12: 11, where "the peaceable fruit of righteousness" is the result of exercise under the hand of God. All is through Jesus Christ, unto the glory and praise of God.

Joy in Gospel Testimony

(chap. 1: 12-20.)

"But I would ye should understand, brethren, that the things which happened unto me have fallen out rather unto the furtherance of the gospel; so that my bonds in Christ are manifest in all the palace [or, Prætorium, *i. e.*, Cæsar's Guard], and in all other places; and many of the brethren in the Lord, waxing confident by my bonds, are much more bold to speak the word without fear. Some indeed preach Christ even of envy and strife; and some also of good will. The one preach Christ of contention, not sincerely, supposing to add affliction to my bonds; but the other of love, knowing that I am set for the defence of the gospel. What then? Notwithstanding, every way, whether in pretence, or in truth, Christ is preached; and I therein do rejoice, yea, and will rejoice. For I know that this shall turn to my salvation through your prayer, and the supply of the Spirit of Jesus Christ, according to my earnest expectation and hope, that in nothing I shall be ashamed, but that with all boldness, as always, so now also Christ shall be magnified in my body, whether it be by life, or by death."

IT is always a sad sign, and an evidence of spiritual decline, when the heart loses its interest

in the message of grace. Some there are so occupied with the deeper truths of the Word of God
that they allow themselves to speak slightingly of
the simplicity of the gospel. Paul was the pre-
eminent teacher of the Church, but to his last
hour, his heart was filled with gospel zeal, and his
sympathies were with the evangelist carrying the
Word of Life to men dead in trespasses and in
sins. Even in his prison-house he rejoiced that
his affairs had really tended to the progress of the
gospel. Satan, doubtless, hoped to hinder that
work by locking up the apostle in a jail, but even
there it became manifest to all Cæsar's court, and
to all others, that his bonds were for Christ's sake.
The very soldiers appointed to guard him were
brought thus to hear the glorious proclamation of
grace to a guilty world; and it is evident, both
from the 13th verse, and the 22nd verse of the
4th chapter, that numbers of them believed. Who
can fathom the joy that must have filled the heart
of Paul as he led one guard after another to the
Saviour's feet! Just as when cast into the Philippian dungeon, he and his companion Silas were
used to the conversion of the jailer and his household, so here, grace triumphed over all seemingly
untoward circumstances, and the prison cell became a gospel chapel, where souls were being born
of God, and stern Roman soldiers became them-

selves the captive servants of One greater than Cæsar.

In the 14th verse the apostle speaks of another cause of joy. While he was going about from place to place preaching the Word, there were gifted men who held back, feeling, perhaps, that they were in no sense on a par with him, and so they permitted the timidity and backwardness of the flesh to hinder their launching out in a work to which the Lord was beckoning them. But now that he is in durance, and can no longer go about from place to place in this happy service, numbers of these men came forward, and, for the Name's sake, went forth preaching the Word boldly, without fear. On the other hand there were some restless men who had not commended themselves as fitted for evangelistic work, and while he was free, were kept in a place of subjection; but now that he was incarcerated they saw their opportunity to come to the front, and went forth preaching Christ indeed with their lips, though their hearts were filled with envy and strife. But no jealous or envious thoughts entered the mind of Paul. He rejoiced in those who preached the Word through good will, out of love, knowing that he was appointed for the vindication of the gospel; and, though he could not rejoice in the spirit that moved the others, he, at

least was gladdened to know that it was Christ
who was being preached. And so he was thankful
for every voice telling out the story of the Cross.
Nor would he permit anything to rob him of this
joy.

How marked is the contrast between the spirit
here exhibited, and that which often prevails to-
day. How seldom, in fact, do we see this simple
unalloyed rejoicing that Christ is preached, let the
aims and methods of the preacher be what they
will. Untold harm is often done by harsh, cap-
tious criticism of young and earnest men, who
often have much to learn, and offend by their un-
couthness, by their lack of discernment and understanding of the ways of the Lord, who nevertheless do preach Christ, and win souls. And God
has said, "He that winneth souls is wise;" or, as
the Revised Version so strikingly puts it, "He that
is wise winneth souls." Often have anxious souls
been really hindered by the criticism of their elders in matters of this kind. Oh, for more of the
spirit of Paul that would lead us to rejoice un-
feignedly whenever Christ is preached, even
though there be much to exercise our hearts and
lead to prayer—and it may be to godly admoni-
tion at times, so far as methods and expressions
are concerned, which if rightly dealt with now,
may soon disappear as excrescences, when the

earnest evangelist grows in grace and in the knowledge of the truth.

The 19th and 20th verses show us how the apostle relied upon the prayers of the people of God, and how encouraged he was by this abounding gospel testimony. He felt that it presaged his own deliverance, and pointed to the time when he would again be free according to his earnest expectation, and hope, to preach Christ openly and widely if it should be the will of God, or else to glorify Him in a martyr's death. He had but one ambition, and that, that Christ Himself should be magnified in his body whether by life or by death. No matter what he himself might be called upon to toil or suffer, if the One whom he had met on that never-to-be-forgotten day on the Damascus turnpike were exalted and honored—this would satisfy him.

It is this utter absence of self-seeking that commends any true servant of Christ. We see it strikingly in John the Baptist, who said, "He must increase, but I must decrease." It should be the one supreme characteristic of the evangelist, pastor, or teacher. And where this spirit of self-abnegation for the glory of the Lord is really found, it must commend the ministry, though it makes nothing of the minister. Oh, that one might enter more fully into it!

Christ is all in Life or Death

(chap. 1: 21-26.)

"For to me to live is Christ, and to die is gain. But if I
live in the flesh, this is the fruit of my labor: yet what I
shall choose I wot not. For I am in a strait betwixt two,
having a desire to depart, and to be with Christ, which is
far better: nevertheless to abide in the flesh is more needful for you. And having this confidence, I know that I
shall abide and continue with you all for your furtherance
and joy of faith; that your rejoicing may be more abundant in Jesus Christ for me by my coming to you again."

"To me to live is Christ" is Christian life and
experience in its fulness. It has often been re-
marked, and is well worth remembering, that
Christians have many experiences which are not
properly Christian experience. The man described
in the 7th of Romans is undergoing an experience
which will be for his future blessing, but it is not
proper Christian experience, though it is clearly
enough the experience of a Christian. Christ Himself, so dominating and controlling the believer,
that his one object is to live to His glory, is what
Paul has before him here. This should be the experience of Christians at all times. But, alas, how
few of us enter into it in its entirety. It implies
a surrendered will, and the body yielded to the
Lord who has redeemed it, that it may be used
only to His praise. This is life in its truest sense,

and, probably, no one ever entered into it so fully as the apostle Paul.

We may, perhaps, better understand the experience, "For me to live is Christ," if we consider for a moment what life means to many an other. The Christless business man, whose one aim and object is to obtain wealth, might well say, "For me to live is money." The careless seeker after the world's pleasures, if he told the truth, would say, "For me to live is worldly pleasure." The carnal voluptuary given up to self-gratification, would say, "For me to live is self." The statesman, exulting in the plaudits of the people, and craving world-notoriety, might truthfully declare, "For me to live is fame and power." But Paul could say, and every Christian should be able to say, "For me to live is Christ."

And it is only such who can heartily add, "And to die is gain." Death is no enemy to the one to whom Christ is all. To *live* gives opportunity to manifest Christ down here; to *die* is to be with Christ, than which nothing could be more precious.

The apostle himself was in a dilemma as to which of these he would prefer, were the choice left to him. If permitted to continue in the body, he would have further opportunity of service for Him who had claimed him as His own and called him to this ministry. But, on the other hand, he longed "to depart and to be with Christ, which is far better." His had been a life of toil and suffering for Christ's sake, such as only a Spirit-sustained man could have endured without fainting; and as he lay in the Roman prison, his heart longed for release—a release which would mean to be forever with Christ. Labor for Christ was sweet, but rest with Christ would be sweeter. Whitefield used to say, "I am often weary *in* the work, but never weary *of* it," and such was, doubtless, the attitude of our apostle. He loved to serve, yet longed too for the hour of release, with no selfish motive in it, for his one object was Christ, whether in life or in death.

It is amazing how anyone, with words such as these before him, could question for a moment that the Word of God teaches the consciousness of the spirit after death. Paul had no thought that his spirit would be buried in the grave with his body, or that his soul would sleep until the resurrection day. Death to him would be a departure, an exodus, a moving out of the travel-worn earthly tabernacle, and a going to be with Christ, until the first resurrection at the coming of the Lord.

As he weighs everything, the unselfishness of the man comes out strikingly. He sees the need of the Church of God. As it is now, so it was then. There were many evangelists, or gospelers, but few teachers and pastors who really carried the people of God upon their hearts; and he felt that to abide in the flesh was more needful for the flock than rest was for himself. So he says he has confidence that he should abide a little longer, and continue in this scene of labor for the furtherance and joy of faith of the people of God.

It is clear, I think, that he fully expected the Lord would permit him to revisit Philippi, that the rejoicings of the saints there might be more abundant in Christ Jesus on his behalf, through his coming to them again. They were his children in the faith: as a tender father he yearned over them, and longed to see them once more before closing his earthly ministry. We have no record in the Word of God as to whether this desire was fulfilled, but there are early church traditions which indicate that it was. At any rate, we know he was released from his first imprisonment, and allowed to go about in freedom for several years before being again apprehended and martyred for the sake of Christ Jesus, his and our Lord, following Him thus even unto death.

Unity in Gospel Testimony

(chap. 1: 27-30.)

"Only let your conversation (or, behavior) be as it becometh the gospel of Christ: that whether I come and see you, or else be absent, I may hear of your affairs, that ye stand fast in one spirit, with one mind striving together for the faith of the gospel; and in nothing terrified by your adversaries: which is to them an evident token of perdition, but to you of salvation, and that of God. For unto you it is given in the behalf of Christ, not only to believe on Him, but also to suffer for his sake: having the same conflict which ye saw in me, and now hear to be in me."

THE word "conversation," as ordinarily employed by our forefathers, was of far wider scope than as generally used by us to-day. It meant not only the talk of the lips, though it included that, but it took in the entire behavior. The apostle's exhortation is to the effect that the whole manner of life of the people of God should be in accordance with the gospel of Christ. No more important message was ever committed to man than the word of reconciliation, which God has graciously entrusted to His people in this present dispensation of His mercy to a lost world. That gospel tells of the divine means of deliverance from the guilt and power of sin. How incongruous, then, if the testimonies of those who undertake to proclaim it with their mouths deny its power in their lives! A walk worthy of the gospel is a walk in the energy of the Holy Spirit; it is a life surrendered to Him, whose Lordship that gospel declares.

But it is not merely our *individual* responsibility to walk worthy of the gospel that the apostle here presses. He has rather before him *assembly* responsibility. He desires to hear of the affairs of the Philippians, that, as an assembly, they stand fast in one spirit with one mind, co-operating vigorously for the faith of the gospel. Nothing so mars gospel testimony as contention and self-seeking among God's people. Where jealousies and envyings come in to hinder the fellowship of those who should be standing together heart to heart and shoulder to shoulder for the truth of God, the effect on the world outside is most lamentable. This is particularly so with the unsaved members of believers' families. Nothing is more harmful to them than to find out that their elders are not commending the message they profess to love, by unitedly standing together for the Word of God.

Is there not something here that deserves the careful consideration of many believers in the assemblies gathered to the name of the Lord Jesus Christ at the present time? Have we not allowed personalities, bickerings, and strife to greatly mar

and hinder gospel testimony? On the other hand,
it must be confessed that some, possessing evangelistic gift, have ignored, to a very marked degree, the importance of assembly fellowship in
gospel testimony, launching forth often without
the prayerful endorsement of older, more godly
saints: they are afterwards surprised and grieved
that they do not find heartier co-operation on the
part of assemblies whose judgment they ignored
to begin with. The evangelist is the Lord's servant, and, therefore, is not subject to human dic-
tation, but, on the other hand, fellowship involves
mutual responsibility, and evangelists need to remember that gift is not necessarily piety, nor does
it always carry with it good judgment and sound
wisdom. Therefore the importance of cultivating
humility on the part of the servant, if he would
have the hearty fellowship of assemblies in his
work.

When there is this lowly, subject spirit manifested by the evangelist, and vigorous co-operation
on the part of the assembly, God can be depended
on to work in mighty power to the salvation of
lost souls, and the blessing of His people; and
this, to the enemy, is a condition he most dreads.
Where an assembly is walking in love, and exercised about the Lord's things in this scene, they
need not fear the attacks of evil powers, natural

or supernatural, from without. These unholy hosts read their own doom in the happy fellowship of the saints of God, and see in it a proof of the truth of the Lord's words, "Upon this rock I will build mine assembly, and the gates of hell shall not prevail against it." The thought that many have in mind in reading this scripture seems to be that the assembly of God is as a city *besieged*, beleaguered by the enemies of the Lord, and carrying on a *defensive* warfare, though with the pledge of eventual victory. This, however, is far from fulfilling the picture presented by our Lord. An invading or besieging army does not carry the gates of its cities with it. It is hell, or hades, the realm of darkness, that is being besieged by the forces of light who are carrying on, not a *defensive*, but an *offensive* warfare, and to them the promise is given that "the gates of hell shall not prevail." This is the "perdition" spoken of in verse 28.

Such fellowship as that which the apostle brings before us, cannot be fully entered into apart from suffering, but this is to be esteemed as a privilege by those who fight under the banner of the risen Lord. It is given to such, as it were a guerdon greatly to be desired, in behalf of Christ Himself, not only to trust in Him as Saviour, but manfully to toil and suffer, that His name may be glorified

in the scene where He Himself was rejected and
crucified, and over which He is soon coming to
reign.

How blessedly and how fully had the apostle
entered into this! With what joy did he endure
and suffer that Christ might be glorified! Yea, at
the very time of writing this letter he was the
prisoner of the Lord in a Roman prison, while
saints at Philippi, some of them at least, were
living in comfort and slothfulness, and some even
stooping to quarreling among themselves. The
apostle's words in verse 30 would prove, surely,
a home-thrust to such as these, stirring heart and
conscience, as they contrasted their easy-going
lives with the sufferings of Christ's dear servant,
who was in prison because of his unselfish devotion to the Lord he loved. May we learn to walk
in the same spirit, and mind the same things!

CHAPTER TWO

CHRIST THE BELIEVER'S EXAMPLE

"Others"

(vers. 1-4.)

"If there be therefore any consolation in Christ, if any comfort of love, if any fellowship of the Spirit, if any bowels and mercies, fulfil ye my joy, that ye be likeminded, having the same love, being of one accord, of one mind. Let nothing be done through strife or vainglory; but in lowliness of mind let each esteem other better than themselves. Look not every man on his own things, but every man also on the things of others."

THE last word of this section is the keynote —"*others.*" This was the overpowering, dominating note in the life of our Lord on earth, and because of this He died. "He came not to be ministered unto, but to minister, and to give his life a ransom for"—*others!* He lived for *others;* He died for *others.* Selfishness He knew not. Unselfish devotion for the good of *others* summed up His whole life, and all in subjection to the Father's will. For God, the Father Himself, lives, reverently be it said, for *others.* He finds His delight, His joy, in lavishing blessing on *others.* He pours His rain, and sends His sunshine upon the just and the unjust alike. He gave His Son for *others;* and having not withheld His own Son, but delivered Him up for us all, how will He not with Him also freely give us all things?—we, who are included in the *others* for whom the Lord Jesus Christ endured so much. What wonder then that, if we would follow His steps, we find ourselves called upon to live for *others*, and even to lay down our lives for the brethren!

In the first verse, the "if" does not imply that there might not be consolation in Christ, comfort of love, and fellowship of the Spirit, coupled with tender mercies toward all for whom Christ died; it rather has the force of *since*—it is an intensive form of saying, Since you know there are consolations and comforts in Christ. If these things are blessed realities, how incongruous for a believer to act as though they were non-existent! Drinking in the spirit of Christ, we exemplify the mind of Christ. And so the apostle exhorts the saints to fulfil his cup of joy by likemindedness among themselves, with equal love toward one another, being of one accord, of one mind.

It is very evident that Christians will never see eye to eye on all points. We are so largely influenced by habits, by environment, by education, by the measure of intellectual and spiritual apprehension to which we have attained, that it is an impossibility to find any number of people who

look at everything from the same standpoint. How
then can such be of one mind? The apostle himself explains it elsewhere when he says, "I think
also that I have the mind of Christ." The "mind
of Christ" is the lowly mind. And, if we are all
of *this* mind, we shall walk together in love, con-
sidering one another, and seeking rather to be
helpers of one another's faith, than challenging
each other's convictions.

This is emphasized in the third verse, "Let nothing be done through strife or vainglory." It is
possible, as verses 15 and 16 of chapter one have
already shown us, to be controlled by this spirit
of strife and vainglory, even in connection with
the holy things of the Lord; but Paul himself has
furnished us a beautiful example of that lowliness
of mind of which he speaks, when he could rejoice
even though Christ were preached in contention.

Nothing is less suited to a follower of the meek
and lowly Son of Man than a contentious spirit,
and vainglorious bearing. Boasting and bitter
words ill become one who has taken the place of
death with Christ. If, in lowliness of mind, each
esteems others better than himself, how impossible for strife and contention to come in. Alas,
that it is so much easier to speak or write of these
things than to practically demonstrate them!

It is not in the natural man to live out what is

here inculcated. The man after the flesh "looks out for number one," as he puts it, and is fond of reminding himself, and his fellows, that "charity begins at home." But the Christian is exhorted to look, not on his own things, but on the things of *others*. A heavenly principle this, surely, and only to be attained by a heavenly man, one who walks in fellowship with Him who came from heaven to manifest His love for *others*. It is characteristic of man's deceitful natural heart to suppose that his greatest pleasure can be found in ministering to his own desires. But the truest happiness is the result of unselfish devotion to the things of *others*. Were this ever kept in mind, what unhappy experiences would many of God's dear children be spared, and how glad and joyous would fellowship in Christ become.

"The Kenosis"

(chap. 2: 5-8.)

"Let this mind be in you, which was also in Christ Jesus: who, being in the form of God, thought it not robbery to be equal with God, but made Himself of no reputation, and took upon Him the form of a servant, and was made in the likeness of men. And being found in fashion as a man, He humbled Himself, and became obedient unto death, even the death of the cross."

WE now come to consider one of the most sublime and wonderful mysteries in all Scripture:

what has been called by theologians, "The Doctrine of the Kenosis." The title comes from the Greek expression, rendered in our Authorized Version, "made Himself of no reputation"—an expression which really means "emptied Himself," or "divested Himself." Its full force will come before us as we proceed with our study.

It is a noticeable thing that doctrines are never presented in Scripture merely as dogmas to be accepted by the faithful on pain of expulsion from the Christian company. The most important doctrines are brought in by the Holy Spirit in what we might call an exceedingly natural way. I do not use the word "natural" here in contrast to "spiritual," but rather in the sense simply of sequence to the subject, introduced without special emphasis. In this particular instance before us, the doctrine of our Lord's self-emptying comes in simply as the supreme illustration of that lowliness of mind which should characterize all who profess to be followers of the Saviour. It follows naturally upon the exhortation of the fourth verse, which we have already considered.

"Let this mind be in you, which was also in Christ Jesus" is the way the subject is introduced. This mind is the lowly mind, as it is written, "Even Christ pleased not Himself." And the exemplification of this is at once abruptly intro-

duced. He existed from all eternity in the form
of God. It is a declaration of His true Deity. No
creature could exist in the form of God. Lucifer
aspired to this, and for his impiety was hurled
down from the archangel's throne. Our Lord Jesus Christ was in the full enjoyment of this by
right, because He was the eternal Son. He thought
equality with God not a thing to be grasped or
held on to. Equal with God He was, but He chose
to take the place of subjection and lowliness. He
chose to step down from that sublime height
which belonged to Him, even "the glory which He
had with the Father before the world was," and
took the servant's form to do the Father's will.

The first man aspired to be as God, and fell.
The second man, the Lord from heaven, came, as
we sometimes sing,

> "From Godhead's fullest glory,
>   Down to Calvary's depth of woe."

He would not retain the outward semblance of
Deity. He relinquished His rightful position to
become the Saviour of sinners. In order to do
this He emptied Himself, or divested Himself, of
His divine prerogatives.

Let there be no mistake as to this. While we
reverently put off our shoes from our feet, and
draw near to behold this great sight, let us not

fear to accept the declaration of Holy Scripture in all its fulness. He divested Himself of something —but of what? Not of His Deity, for that could not be. He was ever the Son of the Father, and, as such, a divine person. He could take manhood into union with Deity, but He could not cease to be Divine. Of what, then, did He divest Himself? Surely of His rights as God the Son. He chose to come to earth to take a place of subjection. He took upon Him the form of a servant, and was made in the likeness of men.

Observe the distinction brought out in these two verses. He existed from all eternity in the form of God. He came here to take the form of a servant. Angels are servants, but "He took not hold of angels," we are told in the epistle to the Hebrews (chap. 2 : 16, *N. Trans.*). He became in the likeness of men. It was all voluntary on His part. And, as a man on earth, He chose to be guided by the Holy Spirit. He daily received from the Father, through the Word of God, the instruction which it became Him, as a Man, to receive. His mighty works of power were not wrought by His own divine omnipotence alone. He chose that they should be wrought in the power of the Holy Spirit. This is the precious and important doctrine of the Kenosis as revealed in Scripture in contrast with the false teaching of men.

Men have added to this what Scripture does *not* say. They have declared that, when He came to earth, He ceased to be God; that He became but an ignorant Galilean peasant. Hence His knowledge of divine mysteries was no greater than what might have been expected of any other good man of His day and generation. Therefore His testimony as to the inspiration of Scripture has no real weight. He did not know more than others of His day knew. He was not competent to speak as to the authors of the Old Testament books. He thought Daniel wrote the book that bears his name, and that Moses penned the Pentateuch. But the wiseacres of to-day do not hesitate to declare that He was wrong, and they base their declaration on the position above taken. He emptied Himself of His divine knowledge they say, therefore He could not speak with authority.

The Exaltation of the Man Christ Jesus
(chap. 2: 9-11.)

"Wherefore God also hath highly exalted Him, and given Him a name which is above every name: that at the name of Jesus every knee should bow, of things in heaven, and things in earth, and things under the earth (or, of heavenly, earthly, and infernal beings), and that every tongue should confess that Jesus Christ is Lord, to the glory of God the Father."

THIS is the glorious fulfilment of the prophecy of the 110th psalm—a prophecy used by our Lord to confound the cavillers of His day, who professed to be waiting for the promised Messiah, but rejected His deity. "Jehovah said unto my Lord, Sit Thou at my right hand, until I make thine enemies thy footstool." He is David's Son— the Branch of David, yet David calls Him Lord, because He is likewise the Root of David. He descended from Jesse's son, yet the son of Jesse came into being through Him. His exaltation as man to the throne of God is not only Jehovah's attestation of perfect satisfaction in His work, but also the recognition of His equality with Himself. This Man, who had so humbled Himself as to go even to the death of the cross, is Jehovah's Fellow, as Zechariah 13 : 7 declares. Of none but a Divine person could such language be rightly used.

It is interesting to notice that God never permitted one indignity to be put upon the body of His Son after His work was finished, as the Roman soldier, having pierced His side, released the atoning blood. No enemies' hands thenceforth touched it. Loving disciples tenderly took it down from the cross, and reverently laid it away in Joseph's new tomb after wrapping it in the linen clothes.

Then, upon the expiration of the time appointed, He who had died came forth in resurrection-life, and God the Father received Him up into glory. He has highly exalted Him, and given Him a name which is above every Name. He is the preeminent one in every sphere. How suited it is that His glory should thus answer to His shame. "*As* many were astonished at Him...*so* shall He astonish many nations" (Isa. 52: 14, 15, *literal rendering*). God has ordained it, and so it must be. At the name of Jesus—His personal name, which means Jehovah-the-Saviour — the name borne upon the title placed above His head as He hung upon the cross — every knee shall bow: heavenly, earthly, and infernal beings—all must own Him Lord of all.

Observe that here, where it is a question of the recognition of His authority, three spheres are brought in, comprising all created intelligent beings—in heaven, earth and hell. There will be no exceptions. All must confess His Lordship to the glory of God the Father. All must bow in lowly submissiveness at the mention of the name of the Crucified.

Does this then imply universal salvation, even the final restoration of Satan and his hosts, as some have taught? Surely not. *Subjugation* is one thing; *reconciliation* is another. When the latter is in question, we have but two spheres mentioned, as in Col. 1: 20: "Having made peace by the blood of his cross, by Him to reconcile all things unto Himself; by Him, I say, whether they be things in earth or things in heaven." There is here no mention of the underworld. The lost will never be reconciled. Heaven and earth will eventually be filled with happy beings who have been redeemed to God by the precious blood of Christ. Then reconciliation will be complete.

But "under the earth" will be those who "have their part" in the outer darkness, the lake of fire. They flaunted Christ's authority on earth. They will have to own it in hell! They refused to heed the call of grace and be reconciled to God in the day when they might have been saved. In the pit of woe no gospel message will ever be proclaimed, but the authority of the Lord Jesus Christ will be supremely enforced there too. There will be no disorder in hell; no further rebellion will be permitted. All must bow at the name of Jesus, and every tongue confess Him Lord. Scripture depicts no wild pandemonium when describing the abode of the lost.

How blessed to own His Lordship now, according as it is written, "That if thou shalt confess with thy mouth Jesus as Lord, and shalt believe in thy heart that God hath raised Him from the dead, thou shalt be saved. For with the heart man believeth unto righteousness; and with the mouth confession is made unto salvation" (Rom.

10 : 9, 10). How fitting it is that such, and such alone, should be eternally saved as a result of the work of the Cross.

"Working out Salvation"

(chap. 2: 12-16.)

"Wherefore, my beloved, as ye have always obeyed, not as in my presence only, but now much more in my absence, work out your own salvation with fear and trembling. For it is God which worketh in you both to will and to do of his good pleasure. Do all things without murmurings and disputings: that ye may be blameless and harmless, the sons of God, without rebuke, in the midst of a crooked and perverse nation, among whom ye shine as lights in the world; holding forth the word of life; that I may rejoice in the day of Christ, that I have not run in vain, neither labored in vain."

HAVING thus occupied the hearts of the saints at Philippi with the self-abnegation of our Lord Jesus Christ, the apostle, as guided by the Holy Spirit, goes on, in the balance of this chapter, to apply the truth in a practical way.

First, the verses now before us refer to assembly-life and responsibility. Then, from verse 17 to the end of this chapter, three men are brought before us who were seeking to manifest in their lives the devotedness and self-denying concern for others that was seen in Christ as a Man on earth.

Verse 12 has often perplexed those who thought they saw clearly from Scripture the simplicity of salvation by grace, apart from works. Here, in seeming contrast to this, the apostle tells the saints to work out their own salvation, and that with fear and trembling, as though possibly there were danger that salvation might be forfeited because of failure in properly working it out.

Notice first, however, that the apostle does not speak of working *for* salvation, but of working it *out*, which is a very different thing. One might instance the quaint saying of the little girl who listened to a legal sermon preached upon this text by a minister who was insisting that none could be saved by grace alone, but all must work out their own salvation. Innocently she asked at the close of the service, "Mother, how can you work it out if you haven't got it in?" If it were individual salvation that is here contemplated, it might be enough to say—it is your own; therefore manifest it — work it out. But there is really more than this. For, taken in its full connection, it will be seen the passage refers to assembly salvation, rather than to the individual: that is, direction is given to an assembly of Christians (exposed to difficulties from without and from within, passing through a world where all is in opposition to the testimony committed to them), showing

them how to go on in fellowship together in spite
of the fact that each individual has within him a
corrupt nature, which will manifest itself to the
detriment of the whole assembly, if given occasion.

We have already noticed that there was some
difficulty in the Philippian assembly, between two
sisters of prominence, Euodia and Syntyche. This
might easily become the occasion for distressing
quarrels, and even division, if not judged in the
presence of the Lord. Similar things might arise
from time to time, and would need to be carefully
watched against. When the apostle himself was
with them, they could refer all such matters to
him, and he would, so to speak, work out their
salvation from these perplexities. He would ad-
vise and guide as needed. Now he is far away, a
prisoner for the gospel's sake, and cannot personally give the help he might desire. He, therefore, directs them in his absence, as obedient children, to work out their own salvation in godly
fear, and with exercise of soul, lest they depart
from the right path, or miss the mind of God.

Viewed from this standpoint, how salutary are
his words for all future generations of Christians!
There is no assembly of saints on earth but will
probably, sooner or later, have its internal differences, and the advice or command here given ap-

plies in just such cases. It is God's way that
assemblies should be put right from within, by
self-judgment in His presence and submission to
His word.

How often do saints take the very opposite
method. Questions arise to trouble and perplex;
differences of judgment occur, and bickerings and
quarrels begin. Instead of coming together in the
presence of God for humiliation and guidance,
seeking His mind from His own Word and acting
accordingly, they apply to this one or that one outside for help—often only to have things worse
complicated. Those engaged in the ministry of
the Word, traveling from place to place, are perhaps appealed to, and requested to adjudicate in
matters which often only disturb their spirits,
and, after all, cannot really effect the salvation of
the assembly from the troubles that have arisen.

It is easy to see how the clerical system arose,
from such experiences. We see in the early
Church, men of the stamp of Diotrephes, who
loved to have the pre-eminence, and Nicolaitanes,
that is, rulers of the people, who sought to bring
the saints into bondage. And, on the other hand,
it was very early made manifest that believers
generally found it much easier to apply to noted
preachers or teachers for help, than to be cast
directly upon God and His Word themselves. Thus

gifted men became a court of appeal, and, eventually, were recognized as "the clergy." The same principle easily creeps in wherever saints look to men rather than to God and His Word. If it be said that they are too ignorant to know how to settle their differences, yet let it be remembered they have God, and the word of His grace; and if there be but humility and waiting upon Him, refusing to move until they find direction in the Book, He can be depended upon to help them work out their own salvation from whatever perplexing circumstances have arisen. He does not cast them upon their own resources, but on His Word, on Himself, who works in them the will to do His good pleasure. This does not mean that they should ignore or despise the advice and sound judgment of others—but they are not dependent upon it.

In verses 14 to 16 we see this working out of assembly salvation practically demonstrated. Murmurings and disputings must be judged in the presence of God. Instead of backbiting, and gossiping about matters, let the saints come together before the Lord, and deal with them in the light of His revealed Word. Thus they shall be blameless and harmless, the sons of God indeed, without rebuke; walking in a manner worthy of the Lord, in the midst of a crooked and perverse generation among whom they shine as lights in this dark world. Thus judging what would hinder fellowship within, they are in a suited condition to be a testimony to the power of grace to those without. And, as the apostle has already emphasized for us in chapter one, nothing so delivers believers from self-occupation as occupation with Christ and the presentation of Christ to those still in their sins. They who are busy holding forth the Word of Life have no time for selfish quarreling amongst themselves.

In so walking, the saints would give joy to the heart of the apostle, and he could rejoice in the day of Christ: that is, it would be manifest at His judgment-seat that his labors in Philippi had not been in vain. The godly order and devoted gospel testimony would together witness to the reality of the work of God in and among them.

Thus we see that "working out our own salvation" is simply submitting to the truth of God after we have been saved, in order that we may glorify Him, whether as individuals or assemblies of saints in the place of testimony. This will be "with fear and trembling" as we realize our liability to err, the faultiness of our understanding and the holiness of the One whom we are called to serve in this scene.

The Mind of Christ Exemplified in the Apostle Paul

(chap. 2: 17, 18.)

"Yea, and if I be offered upon the sacrifice and service of your faith, I joy, and rejoice with you all. For the same cause also do ye joy, and rejoice with me."

THE apostolic writer now goes on to cite, though in an apparently casual way, three examples of men of like passions with their fellow-believers, who have exemplified in their ways the spirit of Christ. The first of these is himself, and of his testimony we shall now speak. The other two are Timothy and Epaphroditus, whose lowly ways and devoted service will occupy us later.

Possibly no other mortal man ever drank into the spirit of Christ so deeply as the great apostle to the Gentiles. Once a proud, haughty Pharisee, glorying in his own righteousness, burning with indignant bigotry against any who pretended to a higher revelation than that given in Judaism, he had been transformed by a sight of the glorified Christ, when, religious persecutor as he was, he was hurrying to Damascus to apprehend any who confessed the name of Jesus. The sight of the once-crucified, but now enthroned Saviour, at God's right hand, was the means of a conversion so radical and so sudden, that probably no other since has been so intense.

From that moment it was the one desire of his soul, over-mastering all else, the inmost yearning of his being, to manifest Christ in all his ways. Yet he was not an absolutely sinless man, nor without the infirmities common to the human race. But he was one who ever sought to judge himself in the light of the Cross of Christ, with the power of Christ resting upon him. His whole philosophy of life is summed up in his fervent words to the Galatians, "But God forbid that I should glory, save in the cross of our Lord Jesus Christ, by whom the world is crucified unto me, and I unto the world" (Gal. 6: 14).

It was in this spirit that he could write to his beloved Philippians, "Yea, and if I be offered (literally "poured out") upon the sacrifice and service of your faith, I joy, and rejoice with you all." He had just told them that his joy in the day of Christ would be to find them approved, as having walked before God in this scene as unrebuked saints earnestly engaged in holding forth the word of life in a dark world: their abundant service and the reward meted out to them, he would look upon as reward to himself. He would thus feel that he had not run in vain, neither labored in vain. He was willing to count all his service as but an adjunct of theirs; to have their labors and devotedness looked upon as the completion of a work of which his was just the beginning.

In order properly to understand this 17th verse, it is necessary to observe carefully what the apostle has in mind. When he says, "If I be poured out upon the sacrifice of your faith," he alludes to the drink-offering. This was a cup of wine, which was poured out upon the burnt-offering, and was typical of the out-pouring of our Lord Jesus Christ's soul unto death; the voluntary surrender of everything that might naturally be expected to contribute to his joys as a man. Wine is the symbol of gladness. What man ever deserved to be happier than the Lord Jesus Christ? To whom was gladness a righteous due, if not to Him? Yet, in infinite grace, He became "a Man of sorrows and acquainted with grief." The burnt-offering spoke of Him in the highest sense as offering Himself without spot to God, but on our behalf. In the sacrificial service, the burnt-offering having been slain was cut in its pieces, was washed with water, then laid in order upon the fire of the altar and wholly consumed. The drink-offering was simply poured out upon it, and in a moment was lost to sight. Now, with this in mind, consider the beauty of the figure the apostle here employs. Whatever service the Philippians might be able to render to the Lord, would be in fellowship with Christ, and thus their devotedness could be viewed as an offering or a sacrifice of a sweet-smelling savor unto God. It was the result of lives surrendered to the Lord, and Paul was willing that his labor should be simply looked upon as the adjunct of theirs; as the drink-offering poured upon the burnt-offering.

What sublime self-abnegation was this! What delight in the labors of others! What absence of that which sometimes is so abhorrent in professed Christian service to-day! Laborers sometimes are jealous of the ministry of others, and envious of a success in which they think they have not shared. There was no such spirit in the apostle Paul. He rejoiced in everything that the Lord did through others, and his jealousy was only for the glory of God.

And so in this he followed Christ, and he could confidently appeal to them to follow him, as he walked in His steps. So he would have them joy and rejoice with him in the mutual devotedness of both.

It is significant that he speaks of himself and his service in this incidental way—in but one verse. When he turns to write of his fellow-laborer, Timothy, and of their messenger, Epaphroditus, how much more he has to say. He could dwell with delight on the labors and service

of others, but when writing of himself, as he tells
us elsewhere, he felt as though he were speaking
as a fool.

Timothy, the Unselfish Pastor
(chap. 2: 19-24.)

"But I trust in the Lord Jesus to send Timotheus shortly
unto you, that I also may be of good comfort, when I know
your state.   For I have no man likeminded, who will naturally care for your state.   For all seek their own, not
the things which are Jesus Christ's.   But ye know the
proof of him, that, as a son with the father, he hath
served with me in the gospel.   Him therefore I hope to
send presently, so soon as I shall see how it will go with
me.   But I trust in the Lord that I also myself shall come
shortly."

PAUL was not only an ardent evangelist, but
he was also the prince of teachers, and, like his
fellow-apostle Peter, a true pastor, or shepherd,
of the flock of Christ.   In this latter respect the
young preacher Timothy was his ardent imitator.
Whatever other gifts he may have had, that special gift which was given him in connection with
the laying on of the elder brethren's hands, when
he went out in the work of the Lord, was probably that of the pastor.   This is perhaps one of the
rarest, and yet one of the most needed, of all the
gifts given by an ascended Christ for the edification of His Church.   The evangelist ministers to
those without Christ; the teacher instructs those

already saved; the pastor is more concerned about the state of soul of the believer than as to his knowledge of abstract truth, though recognizing, of course, that saints are formed by the truth, and that a right state of soul and a walk in the truth go together.

Paul, therefore, was anxious to send Timothy to Philippi, that he might be a help and a means of blessing to the assembly there, trusting that he might be used of God to weld their hearts into one, and deliver them from the dissensions that had come in through the misunderstanding between Euodia and Synteche. He felt that he could depend on Timothy's judgment, and he counted on being himself comforted when he actually knew their state.

As often pointed out by others, and clearly developed in different parts of Scripture, our standing before God is one thing, our actual state is another. It was as to the latter that Paul was concerned. He did not know of anyone else with the same unselfish shepherd-heart as Timothy, who would whole-souledly care for their state. The word "naturally" does not adequately give the thought. Timothy's pastoral concern was not a gift of nature, but a spiritual one, the result of exercise of soul before God; and his whole soul was stirred with concern for the Lord's people.

Of others, however gifted in various ways, the apostle could only sadly say, "They seek their own, and not the things which are Jesus Christ's."

It is quite possible to be an admired teacher, upon whose words thousands hang, or an eloquent evangelist with eager multitudes flocking to listen with delight to his messages, and yet be a vain self-seeker, using the very gift that God has given, for personal aggrandizement, or to obtain wealth, even while professing to care little or nothing for money. But the more marked the pastoral gift, of very necessity the more unselfishly devoted must the servant be. It will be his great ambition to feed the flock and shield them from their dangers.

The patriarch Jacob is an apt illustration of the true shepherd. Despite all his failures, and the fact that he was largely under the discipline of God through the greater part of his life, he was, nevertheless, a lover of the flock, and ever considerate of their interests. Speaking to Laban, his father-in-law, he could honestly say, as he looked back over his years of caring for the sheep, "Thus I was; in the day the drought consumed me, and the frost by night; and my sleep departed from mine eyes" (Gen. 31: 40). And in expostulating with his brother Esau, who would have him hurry on with all his host, he says, "My lord knoweth that the children are tender, and the flocks and herds with young are with me: and if men should overdrive them one day, all the flock will die" (Gen. 33: 13). A Diotrephes might try to cajole or coerce the flock into submission to his own imperious will, but a God-appointed shepherd will seek to lead on safely, wearing himself out for the blessing of others—not seeking to impress his own will, but to serve the Lord, and to exalt Him.

As a son with a father, Timothy had commended himself to the aged apostle, serving with him in the gospel in all lowliness and humility. Youth is often exceedingly energetic, and impatient of restraint. Age is inclined, perhaps, to be overcautious and slow in coming to conclusions, and it often is a great difficulty for two, so wide apart in years as Paul and Timothy, to labor together happily. But where the younger man manifests the spirit that was in Timothy, and the elder seeks only the glory of God and the blessing of His people, such fellowship in service becomes indeed blessed.

Having thus proven himself, Paul could trust Timothy on a mission such as that upon which he was about to send him. He was waiting to learn the outcome of his appeal to Cæsar, and then he hoped to send him on to Philippi to be a healer of dissensions, and thus a means of cheer and con-

solation to the assembly. Timothy followed Paul
as he followed Christ; he thus became the second
in this company of men who were worthy to be
held up as examples of those who manifested the
mind of Christ.

It was the apostle's desire and hope to follow
later himself and again visit his beloved Philippians; but whether this yearning was ever fulfilled we perhaps shall never know, until all is
manifested at the judgment-seat of Christ. Precious is the faith that can leave all with Him, assured that His ways are always perfect—always
best!

Epaphroditus, the Devoted Messenger
(chap. 2: 25-30.)

"Yet I supposed it necessary to send to you Epaphroditus, my brother, and companion in labor, and fellow-sol-
dier, but your messenger, and he that ministered to my
wants. For he longed after you all, and was full of
heaviness, because ye had heard that he had been sick.
For indeed he was sick, nigh unto death: but God had
mercy on him; and not on him only, but on me also, lest
I should have sorrow upon sorrow. I sent him therefore
the more carefully, that, when ye see him again, ye may
rejoice, and that I may be the less sorrowful. Receive
him therefore in the Lord with all gladness; and hold
such in reputation; because for the work of Christ he
was nigh unto death, not regarding his life, to supply
your lack of service toward me."

IT was Epaphroditus who had brought the
bounty of the Philippian saints to Paul, their

father in Christ. Burning with love towards the Lord's dear servant who was shut up in prison for the gospel's sake, he took the long journey from Macedonia to Rome, the world's metropolis (whether by land or sea we have now no means of knowing), in order to assure him of the love and esteem of the assembly, and relieve his necessities by their gift.

Having accomplished his purpose, he fell sick, possibly overcome by the Roman fever, so dangerous to strangers unacclimated. That his illness was a protracted one is evident, for, ere he became convalescent, time enough had elapsed for word of his condition to reach the Philippians, and for a return message to get back to him, expressing their solicitude for his health and anxiety that he be restored to them again. It is touching to notice that Epaphroditus himself did not seem to be nearly so much concerned about his own illness as he was that it had been the cause of sorrow to them. He was one of those thoroughly self-denying men whose motto might well be expressed in the one word upon which we have already dwelt, "Others."

Now that he was well again he was anxious to be on his way, in order that he might comfort the assembly by his presence among them again, and by bringing to them this Philippian epistle, though it must have been hard for him to leave the apostle still a prisoner. It is evident from verse three of chapter four that he acted as amanuensis in the writing of this letter, which precious parchment he carried to Philippi, and thus preserved it for us and for all saints to the end of time—yea, and we may say forever!

Of Epaphroditus we know nothing save what is here recorded, unless, as some think, he is to be identified with the Epaphras mentioned in the epistle to the Colossions. Epaphroditus means "favored of Aphrodite"—the Greek goddess of love and beauty, answering to the Roman Venus. This makes it manifest that he was of heathen parentage, but he had been brought to know Christ. Epaphras is said to be a diminutive of the same word with the name of the heathen goddess omitted, and therefore simply meaning "graced" or "favored."

Having been won to Christ, he was characterized by a godly zeal to make Him known to others, and to build up and lead on those already saved. He was the exemplification of the mind of Christ as set forth in the beginning of this chapter. He may not have been physically strong; but, at any rate, he was a man who did not spare himself; and for the work of Christ he was sick, nigh unto death. It is evident that sickness is not always the result of sin, as some have taught. In the case of this devoted man of God, it was the result of his self-denying activity on behalf of those to whom he ministered. His illness was the cause of deep sorrow to Paul himself, and, no doubt, led to much prayer on his behalf, and God answered, showing mercy, and raised him up.

Let it be noted that the apostle did not consider he had any right to demand physical healing even for so faithful a laborer as Epaphroditus. Paul recognized it as simply the mercy of God, not as that to which saints have a right. This is true divine healing. And let it be remembered that sickness may be as really from God as health. It is clear that Paul never held or taught "healing in the atonement," and therefore the birth-right privilege of all Christians. Nor do we ever read of him or his fellow-laborers being miraculously healed. Paul himself, Trophimus, Timothy and Epaphroditus, all bear witness to the contrary. The apostle urges the saints to receive their messenger, when he should return to them, with all gladness, and commands them to hold such in reputation, because for the work of Christ he had been sick, nigh unto death, not regarding his life in order to serve Paul in their stead.

Such are the men whom God delights to honor. Like the Lord Jesus, Epaphroditus made himself of no reputation, and because of his very lowliness he is to be held in reputation. The man who holds himself as one worthy of honor and esteem is not the one whom God calls upon the saints thus to recognize; but he who is willing to take the lowly path, seeking not great things for himself, is the man whom the Lord will exalt in due time.

Salutary lessons are thus manifested in all these three devoted men of God, upon whose self-denying ways we have meditated. May we have grace to follow them as they followed Christ!

CHAPTER THREE

CHRIST, THE BELIEVER'S OBJECT, AND THE STEADFAST MIND

"Rejoice"

(vers. 1-3.)

"Finally, my brethren, rejoice in the Lord. To write the same things to you, to me indeed is not grievous, but for you it is safe. Beware of dogs, beware of evil workers, beware of the concision. For we are the circumcision, which worship God in the Spirit, and rejoice in Christ Jesus, and have no confidence in the flesh."

CAREFUL students of the epistles of Paul cannot but notice a peculiarity that frequently occurs in them. Having concluded the main part of his treatise, he seems about to come to an abrupt conclusion, then suddenly is moved by the Spirit of God to launch out into an altogether different line of things, which comes in as a kind of a parenthesis, ere he actually finishes his letter. An instance of this may be seen in the epistle to the Ephesians by comparing the first verses of chapters three and four. It is plain that all of chapter three, after verse one, comes in parenthetically, and in chapter four he concludes what he started to say. Here in Philippians we have a similar case: "Finally, my brethren," he writes, "rejoice in the Lord;" and yet, when we come to chapter 4: 8, where he introduces his closing remarks, we again have the same expression: "Finally, brethren." All of chapter 3 is a new subject, which, as we might think, he had no intention of discussing until pressed by the Holy Spirit to bring in a message for which we can truly thank God, as we would have lost much precious ministry had it been omitted.

It has often been said that this letter is the epistle of joy, and indeed it is. The apostle himself writes with his own heart filled with the joyful recollection of his past experiences in connection with those scenes so dear to him, and he desires them to fulfil his joy, to share with him in the gladness that was his in Christ; and so we have this brief exhortation, "Rejoice in the Lord." Circumstances may at times be anything but conducive to either peace or gladness, yet the trusting soul can always look above the fitful scenes of earth to the throne where Christ sits exalted as Lord at God's right hand. He is over all. There are no second causes with Him. "Shall there be evil in the city and the Lord hath not done it?" asks the prophet. It is "evil," not in the sense of *sin,* of course, but of *calamity,* even if that calamity be the result of sin; nevertheless, it cannot come save as permitted by the Lord. And know-

ing that "All things work together for good to
those who love God, who are the called according
to His purpose," why should the believer either
doubt or fear? Waves may roll high; stormy
winds may beat tempestuously; all to which the
heart had clung may seem to be swept away; but
Christ abides unchanged and unchangeable, the
everlasting portion of those who trust His grace.

We read on one occasion how David, when the
people spoke of stoning him because of a calami-
tous event for which they held him largely responsible, "encouraged himself in the Lord his God."
"The joy of the Lord is your strength," Nehemiah
reminded the remnant of Israel; and ere return-
ing to the Father's house from which He came,
the Lord Jesus imparted His joy to the trembling
company of His disciples. Therefore it is not
only the Christian's privilege, but we may even
say, his duty, to constantly rejoice in the Lord.
Holiness and happiness are intimately linked together.

And yet how often we need to be reminded of
this; as our apostle does here: "To write the same
things to you to me indeed is not irksome, but for
you it is safe." It is well that we should frequently be exhorted to "rejoice in the Lord."

But now the mind of the Spirit refers to another line of things entirely. For our busy enemy

has so many agencies through which he seeks to rob us of that joy in the Lord which is our rightful portion, that three times over in the second verse we have the significant word "beware."

"Beware of dogs." The Jew used this opprobrious title when speaking of the Gentiles who did not bear in their bodies the mark of the Abrahamic covenant. But in the prophet Isaiah, God uses the term to distinguish false pastors or shepherds in Israel: "His watchmen are blind: they are all ignorant, they are all dumb dogs, they cannot bark; sleeping, lying down, loving to slumber. Yea, they are greedy dogs which can never have enough, and they are shepherds that cannot understand: they all look to their own way, every one for his gain, from his quarter" (Isa. 56: 10, 11). And it is plain that when the apostle Peter says, " The dog has turned to his own vomit again," it symbolizes the false religious teacher going back to the things he once professed to abhor.

Now the Philippians, like the early Christians in general, were peculiarly exposed to the ravages of such "dogs." Evil teachers they were, from Judaism, among the flock of Christ, with the purpose of perverting the saints, and leading them back into bondage; and that for their own selfish ends; they are here, by the Holy Spirit, designated by this opprobrious term. They were introducing themselves among the assemblies of God to rend the flock of Christ, that they might have special recognition as leaders in the new company. Professing to be ministers of Christ, they were in reality servants of Satan, as their works proved. No heart have they for the afflicted sheep and lambs for whom Christ died. They would feed themselves, and not the flock, and their judgment is assured.

Consequently he adds, "Beware of evil workers." We need not necessarily distinguish the evil workers from the dogs, for false teachers, whatever their profession of righteousness, are, nevertheless, workers of iniquity. Another figure employed by the Lord in referring to the same general class, is that of "wolves in sheeps' clothing"—deceiving, misleading, destroying, working havoc among those who confess Christ's precious name. Legality, while professing to have in view greater righteousness than that produced by grace, yet proves to be, as the law itself is, simply "the strength of sin" (see 1 Cor. 15: 56).

"Beware of the concision," says the apostle — *i. e.*, mere mutilators of the body. It is a contemptuous term he uses to designate those who taught that the observance of circumcision was imperative to give one a full standing before God.

The apostle will not allow that the mere ordinance
is really circumcision. The only true circumcision since the Cross is, not a carnal ordinance,
but the putting off of the sins of the flesh—the
heart-recognition of the fact that the flesh has
been put to death in the cross of Christ. It is
only as the soul enters into this, and uses the
sharp knife of self-judgment upon the flesh, that
one is delivered from its power.

The mere externalists, including legalists and
ritualists of all descriptions, always make more
of ordinances and outward forms than of the condition of the soul and the spiritual truths sym-
bolized by those ordinances. In Israel we may see
this in the fullest way. They boasted themselves
of their connection with the temple of the Lord,
and gloried in ordinances and legal observances,
while actually far from God and under His dis-
approval. Nor should Christians forget that it is
just as possible for believers now to be occupied
with ordinances and church position, while forgetting the more important things of true piety and
self-judgment. Nothing that God has commanded
is unimportant; but our Lord said to the Jews of
His times, concerning their intense regard for
ordinances and neglect of justice and mercy,
"These ought ye to have done, and not to have
left the other undone."

In the third verse, we have four distinct statements made, which we do well to consider in detail.

First: "We are the circumcision," that is, we are those who have accepted by faith the end of all flesh in the cross of Christ. We recognize its utter corruption and its powerlessness for service to God, even though placed under the most careful training and supervision. We have, therefore, put it off in the cross of Christ, "Where there is neither Greek nor Jew, circumcision nor uncircision, Barbarian, Scythian, bond nor free; but Christ is all, and in all" (Col. 3: 11). We began with God by accepting the mark of judgment upon the flesh; we do not now look for anything good in it, but triumph only in Christ.

Second: "We worship by the Spirit of God." The worship of the old dispensation was largely of a ritualistic character, but the Lord Jesus told the Samaritan woman, "The hour is coming, and now is, when the true worshipers shall worship the Father in spirit and in truth." Outward forms and services, music and genuflections, do not constitute worship. They may even be hindrances to it. Real worship is that of the heart, when the Spirit of God takes of the things of Christ and shows them unto us. As we are occupied with

Him, true praise and adoration ascend to the Father.

Third: "We glory in Christ Jesus." Our boast is in the Lord. We are, ourselves, utterly unprofitable, having nothing about us to commend us to Him who, in grace, has saved us. All our boast is in His loving-kindness and His mighty power exercised in mercy on our behalf.

Lastly he adds: "We have no confidence in the flesh." The flesh of the believer is no more to be trusted than the flesh of the vilest sinner. Regeneration is not a changing of flesh into spirit; nor is that sanctification in which we stand before God a gradual process of such a change within us. "That which is born of the flesh is flesh, and that which is born of the Spirit is spirit." The fleshly nature is never improved, and the new nature received in new birth does not require improvement. "The carnal mind is not subject to the law of God, neither indeed can be." And the spiritual mind is the mind of Christ. It is as we walk in the Spirit that we are delivered from the desires of the flesh. But even after years of godly living, the flesh itself is not one whit better than it was at the very beginning of our Christian life. Therefore, we dare not trust it, knowing that, however blessed the work of God is in our souls, "in our flesh dwells no good thing."

Self-confidence set aside for Christ

(chap. 3: 4-7.)

"Though I might also have confidence in the flesh. If any other man thinketh that he hath whereof he might trust in the flesh, I more: circumcised the eighth day, of the stock of Israel, of the tribe of Benjamin, a Hebrew of the Hebrews; as touching the law, a Pharisee; concerning zeal, persecuting the church; touching the righteousness which is in the law, blameless. But what things were gain to me, those I counted loss for Christ."

PAUL'S own experience comes in aptly to enforce the expression used in verse three, as to which we have been speaking. He had learned experimentally the utter unprofitableness of the flesh. Looked at from a human standpoint, he had far more to glory in before he was converted to Christ than any of the "concision" among the Philippians could possibly have even afterwards. If any had ground for confidence in the flesh, or thought he had, Paul could say, "I more." For they, to whom he wrote, were Gentiles according to natural birth, and, therefore, strangers to the covenants of promise, aliens, and without the true God in the world.

But it was otherwise with the apostle. He was born within the circle of the covenant. He bore upon his body the mark that he was within the sphere of the Abrahamic promise— he was circumcised on the eighth day, and thus marked off from the Gentile world. Nor were his parents "proselytes of the gate," as Gentiles were called who had forsaken idolatry, and, turning to the God of Abraham, Isaac and Jacob, had come within the blessings of the covenant through this rite. He, Paul, was of the stock of Israel; for generations back his family had belonged to the covenant people. Then, too, he was descended, not from a bond-woman but from the favorite wife of Jacob. Moreover, when the ten tribes revolted and turned away from the house of David, the particular tribe from which he sprung, that of Benjamin, had remained true to Jehovah's centre and loyal to the true kingly line. For though Benjamin had failed grievously in the days of the Judges, so that they were like to have been exterminated out of Israel, yet afterwards, through enabling grace, they remained steadfast in the face of grave departure, and thus won for themselves an immortal name. To be a Benjamite was something in which the flesh might well pride itself.

And as to positive religious conviction, Saul of Tarsus had been a Hebrew of the Hebrews. He was no mere Jew by birth, as some who are indifferent to their Hebrew faith. To the very core

of his being he was a follower of the first Hebrew, Abraham himself. As touching the law,
he was in practice, faith, and name, a Pharisee.
Of the various Jewish sects existing in his day,
the Pharisees were the most intensely orthodox,
and clung most tenaciously not only to the revealed word of God, but to a vast body of human
traditions which had been handed down from
their forefathers, and had become in their eyes
as sacred as the written Word itself. It is true that
our Lord describes many of them as hypocrites,
but on the other hand, when He wishes to empha-
size the need of positive righteousness, He says,
"Except your righteousness exceeds that of the
scribes and Pharisees ye shall in no wise enter
into the kingdom of heaven." He would not have
thus spoken if it were not well known that the
Pharisees insisted on obedience to the law of
God; and Paul himself said, on another occasion,
"After the most straitest sect of our religion, I
lived a Pharisee." He lived what he professed,
and that was Judaism of the strictest kind.

His zeal for the traditions of the elders was
seen in the fact that he was a relentless persecutor of the newly-born assembly of God. "Exceedingly mad against them," as he himself confessed, he "persecuted them unto strange cities,"
and even "compelled them to blaspheme." Yet

there is no evidence that he was naturally a man of fierce and implacable disposition. In fact, the words of the glorified Lord, "It is hard for thee to kick against the goads," would seem to imply the contrary.* What he did, he did from a stern sense of duty, not as the fulfilment of his natural desires. Touching the righteousness which the law demanded, he was outwardly blameless. He tells us in the 7th of Romans that of all the commandments there was only one which really convicted him of sin, and the violation of that one commandment, there was no external way of detecting. Who that looked upon the stalwart champion of Jewish orthodoxy could see the covetousness that was in his heart? His outward life gave no evidence of it. Therefore he could speak of himself as blameless.

But when this religious bigot, this stern unyielding champion of what he believed to be the truth of God, was brought into contact with the glorified Christ—that never-to-be-forgotten day

---

*Does not the expression imply, however, that Saul had *fought* against the testimonies to his conscience?—such as Stephen's, whose face they saw "shining as an angel's" while testifying before the council of the Jews, yet to whose death Saul gave his vote, keeping the garments of those that stoned him. And how many other appeals to his conscience, if not to his heart, there must have been as he beat and dragged men and women to prison, compelling them to blaspheme Jesus, if possible!—[ED.

on the Damascus turn-pike—he realized in one
moment the fact declared by the prophet that "all
our righteousnesses are as *filthy rags*." And these
things which were gain to him—these things on
which he had been building his hopes for eternity
—these things which gave him a standing before
the eyes of his fellows and caused them to look
upon him with admiration, he now saw in their
true light—as utterly worthless and polluted garments, unfit to cover him before the eyes of a
holy God, and deserving only to be cast away.
Therefore he exclaims, "What things were gain
to me, those I counted loss for Christ."

Let it be carefully noted that he did not count
them loss merely for Christianity.   In other
words, he was not simply exchanging one religion
for another; it was not one system of rites and
ceremonies giving place to a superior system; or
one set of doctrines, rules and regulations making way for a better one.   Often this has been all
that conversion has meant.   Many people have
thought that "changing their religion" was all
that God required of them.   But it was otherwise
with Saul.   He had come into actual contact with
a divine Person, the once crucified, but now glorified Christ of God.   He had been won by that Person forever, and for His sake he counted all else
but loss. If any fall short of this, they are missing

entirely the point here emphasized. Christ, and Christ alone, meets every need of the soul. His work has satisfied God, and it satisfies the one who trusts in Him. By resting in Christ, confidence in the flesh is forever at an end. All confidence is in Him who died and rose again, and who ever liveth to make intercession for us.

Paul's Steadfast Purpose

(chap. 3: 8-11.)

"Yea, doubtless, and I count all things to be loss for the excellency of the knowledge of Christ Jesus my Lord: for whom I have suffered the loss of all things, and do count them but refuse that I may win Christ, and be found in Him, not having mine own righteousness which is of the law, but that which is through the faith of Christ, the righteousness which is of God by faith; that I may know Him and the power of his resurrection, and the fellowship of his sufferings, being made conformable unto his death; if by any means I might attain unto the out-resurrection from among the dead" (last part, literal rendering).

IT should be noted that many years of faithful witness-bearing intervene between verse 7, which closed our last section, and verse 8, which opens this. Not only had Paul counted all things but loss for Christ when first he saw His glory on the road to Damascus, but the long arduous years since had brought in no change as to this. He

still counted all things to be of no worth as com-
pared with that which had so dazzled the vision
of his soul—the excellency of the knowledge of
Christ Jesus the Lord. How different it is with
many: fervent and self-sacrificing in their first
love, how soon the fine gold of their devotedness
becomes dimmed and their early freshness passes
away! The world, which once seemed so worthless in view of the matchless glory shining in the
face of the Saviour, begins again to exercise at-
tractive power when the heart has "begun to wax
wanton against Christ." It was blessedly otherwise with our apostle. Never for one moment
did he go back on the great renunciation he had
made when first won for that exalted Jesus whom
he had ignorantly persecuted.

And so in this section of the epistle he re-
affirms the faith with which he began. He still
counted all that earth could offer as dross and
refuse when placed alongside of Christ's surpass-
ing glory, which was the one great object ever before him. And this was not with him mere mys-
tical rhapsodizing, for already had he suffered the
loss of all things, even of liberty itself, as we
know (though in these verses he does not refer
to it), and this was all in accord with the domin-
ant purpose of his life, that he might win Christ
and be found in Him in the great consummation.

It is not that he is putting the "being found in Christ" on the ground of attainment, or as something to be earned by self-abnegation, but he is letting us into the secret of the supreme emotion of his being. It is as though he were saying, "Ever since I saw Christ in the glory of God I have considered nothing else as worth living for. He has so won my heart that nothing now counts with me but the blessedness of knowing Him, of being completely identified with Him both in life and in death, yea, and beyond death. I would not stand before God in a righteousness of my own now if I could. I desire only to be found in Him. I long only to know Him more intimately, let the suffering involved be what it may; I would even die as He died at last, if need be—any way that He may choose, that at last, whatever way may lead me to it, I shall attain to the great rapture of all saints at His coming, the glorious out-resurrection from among the dead. This for me will be the goal attained which has been for so long before my soul; for then I shall be so completely identified with Him who has won my heart to Himself, that I shall be like Him forever, and with Him through all the ages to come."

I have sought thus to paraphrase his words in order that it may be clearly seen that there is here no element of uncertainty involved in them, as

many have supposed, and some have taught. He
did not fear that he might miss the first resurrection through unfaithfulness or lack of watchful-
ness. Nor was this out-resurrection from among
the dead a matter of present experience (as the
verses following show), but refers to ·that one
great event for which every instructed Christian
should wait with eagerness—the coming of the
Lord Jesus Christ and our gathering together unto Him.

To teach that the rapture is only for certain devoted saints, and that even Paul himself was
haunted with the fear that he would come short
of it, would be to lose entirely the sense of the
rich grace of God, which is to work in us that
glorious change which will make us like Him
for whom we wait. The uniform teaching of the
apostle is that "they that are Christ's" shall rise
"at His coming." And in this hope the aged prisoner of the Lord faced the prospect of martyr-
dom in its most cruel form. It would be but the
appointed means by which he should attain unto
the blessedness of the first resurrection.

Nor, it seems to me, can we with propriety say
that what the apostle has in mind is the power
of resurrection-life working in him here on earth
so that he may live in the first-resurrection experience, as some have designated it. This would

be dangerously near to the "death to nature"
theories promulgated by earnest but misled men in
the last century, and which resulted in grave
departures from sobriety and scriptural order.
None had more fully entered into that knowledge
of "the power of His resurrection" in his human
body than did the apostle, yet he puts the having
part in the out-resurrection as the climax of all
his years of devoted service. Everything would
be incomplete without that. Nor do I know of
any other place in the word of God where the expression is used as referring to a believer's experience. In fact there is added here a second
preposition to intensify the thought of a selec-
tive resurrection; otherwise it is the regular expression which distinguishes the first resurrection from the second which brings up the remain-
ing dead for judgment (Rev. 20: 4, 5).

That there are two resurrections*— not one
general rising of saved and unsaved at one time—
I take it for granted is clear to my readers, as so
much has been written and orally taught upon
this subject in recent years. The resurrection of
the just; the resurrection of life; the first resurrection; the resurrection from, or out of, the dead

---

* If any are perplexed as to this, may I recommend "The
Two Resurrections, and the Judgment," by C. H. M.—from
the same publishers, 5 cts.

—these are all terms synonymous with the one the apostle uses here.

It is with the eye and heart set upon this that the apostle can cast aside as so much *impedimenta* all that would cause him to glory in the flesh, or give others an occasion to glory on his behalf. Like the racer stripped for the contest, he struggles ardently on with his eye upon the goal, which is for him this out-resurrection. In view of it, suffering cannot daunt him, nor death terrorize him. He sees in both but an opportunity for fuller, sweeter fellowship with his Lord. He would count it all joy to drink of His cup of suffering, and to share in His baptism of death—the last of course only as witness-bearer, as was promised to James and John before him.

How little do most of us enter into this holy "fellowship of His sufferings!" It is to be feared that some who make greatest pretension as to fellowship in things ecclesiastical, would be found sadly wanting when opportunity is given to enter into this fellowship of sorrow and of pain, in which, as in no other phase of fellowship, the soul enters into communion with Him who was on earth a Man of sorrows and acquainted with grief.

Perfection in Two Aspects

(chap. 3: 12-16.)

"Not as though I had already attained, either were already perfect: but I follow after, if that I may apprehend that for which also I am apprehended of Christ Jesus. Brethren, I count not myself to have apprehended; but this one thing I do, forgetting those things which are behind, and reaching forth unto those things which are before, I press toward the mark for the prize of the high calling of God in Christ Jesus. Let us therefore, as many as be perfect, be thus minded: and if in anything ye be otherwise minded, God shall reveal even this unto you. Nevertheless, whereto we have already attained, let us walk by the same rule, let us mind the same thing."

VERY early in the history of the Church men arose who confounded certain spiritual experiences, real or fancied, with the teaching of the Lord Himself and His apostles in regard to the first resurrection. We know of two by name, Hymenæus and Philetus, of whom Paul wrote to Timothy that they had erred concerning the truth, "saying that the resurrection is past already," and by this overthrew the faith of some. Nothing is more detrimental to Christian testimony than making high claims which cannot be substantiated by experience—as some who take the ground of sinlessness, or of the eradication of an evil nature, because their teachers instructed them that this is their privilege as Christians. If after-experience proves that it is impossible to maintain this practically, there is grave danger that they will become utterly disheartened, and possibly renounce the faith entirely, unless preserved by divine grace.

The apostle, therefore, is careful to make it clear that he did not claim to have reached a state of resurrection-perfectness while here upon earth. He uses a word, in this instance, which means completeness, that to which nothing can be added. This state, he declares, he had not already attained. But he had it in view, for he knew that, at the coming of the Lord Jesus Christ, he would be made like Himself, and thus forever free from all tendency to sin. Meantime, he could but follow after, seeking earnestly to lay hold of that for which Christ Jesus had laid hold of him, and in a devoted life to exemplify the power of Christ's resurrection, in which he shared. The 13th and 14th verses might, perhaps, better be rendered as follows: "Brethren, I count not myself to have apprehended; but this one thing, forgetting those things which are behind and reaching forth unto those things which are before, I press toward the mark for the prize of the calling of God on high in Christ Jesus." What he says is that there is only one thing he professes to have apprehended, or laid hold of, namely, that the

path of blessing is found in forgetting the things
that are past, and seeking to lay hold, practically,
of his portion in Christ from day to day while
ever keeping the goal in view. To do this is to
"follow holiness, apart from which no man shall
see the Lord." It is a great mistake to teach that
this verse means that unless one attains to certain
experiences in holy living he will be forever de-
barred from a sight of the Lord; it impresses the
fact upon us, rather, that he who will see the Lord
is one who follows that which characterized his
Master here—an inward and outward separation
from all that is contrary to the mind of God.

The calling of God on high, is that *heavenly*
calling which is characteristic of the present dispensation of grace. Christ is no longer on earth,
His world-kingdom has not yet been set up, but
believers are linked with Him as the glorified Man
at God's right hand, and they are called to re-
present Him in this scene. The prize is the reward
conferred by His own hand at the end of the race,
and toward this Paul was pressing on, counting as
dross and refuse all that would hinder his progress.

To his fellow-believers he says, "Let us, therefore, as many as be perfect, be thus minded."
Are we then to understand that there is real or
implied contradiction here to what has gone be-

fore? He has told us that he was *not* perfect.
Here he speaks as though he were, and links
others with him in this perfection. The fact is,
a somewhat different word is here used from that
of verse 12. It implies perfection in *growth*—in
development. An apple in June may be a perfect
apple, so far, but it will have much greater completeness, or perfection in that sense, in August
or September. And so with the believer.

The perfection of verse 15 is that of full
growth, answering somewhat, if not altogether,
to the "fathers" of 1st John, chap. 2. Such have
eschewed the world and its follies. Christ has become to them the *one Object* before the soul. To
live for Him and seek His glory is the only thing
that counts in their estimation. And yet such
saints are still compassed with infirmity. They
are likely to err in judgment; they may make
grave mistakes, and come to wrong conclusions—
influenced as we are by early education, by environment, by mental capacity—and may even be
misled as to doctrinal questions. Nevertheless,
theirs is the mind of Christ, and they may be
comforted by the added words of the apostle that,
"If in anything ye be otherwise minded, God shall
reveal even this unto you."

Where there is a willingness to be taught of
God, the illuminating grace of the Holy Spirit can

be depended upon to open up His Word, and guide into all truth. But he would be a bold man indeed, who would dare to say, "I understand all truth, all mysteries are clear to me. I have a perfect apprehension of the divine revelation." Only the boldest egotism could lead anyone to take such ground. How patient, therefore, we need to be with one another; how ready to confess that we know but in part, and to recognize the fact that we are ever in need of further instruction. "Nevertheless, whereto we have already attained, let us walk by the same rule, let us mind the same thing." There are truths and principles so plainly put in God's Word, that any Spirit-taught believer may readily see them.

Where these truths are learned, it is our responsibility to walk in them—walk *together* in them, as far as possible, counting on God to reveal to us whatever may be lacking, as we patiently and prayerfully learn from Him through His Word. A wider recognition of these things would lead to more kindly consideration of one another, and tend to make us helpers of each other's faith, rather than judges of a brother's doubtful thoughts.

Enemies of the Cross of Christ

(ch. 3: 17-19.)

"Brethren, be followers together of me, and mark them which walk so as ye have us for an example. (For many walk, of whom I have told you often, and now tell you even weeping, that they are the enemies of the cross of Christ; whose end is destruction, whose God is their belly, and whose glory is in their shame, who mind earthly things)."

THE sentence is incomplete and needs the verses that follow to conclude it properly; but I have purposely left it so that we may consider this portion of it the more carefully, for the next part has to do with another and altogether happier theme. Here, the apostle is occupying us with the responsibilities and snares of the pilgrim path; there, he points us on to the goal when all danger will be forever past, and with it all opportunity to bear faithful testimony to a rejected Lord in a scene of contrariety. How it behoves us to consider the brevity of the time allotted us for witness-bearing! It will soon be forever too late to *suffer* for and with Christ, and this necessarily means too late to win an honored place in the everlasting kingdom of our Saviour-God. That which we call "time" is the training-school for

the ages to come. What a mistake to fritter away
its precious moments—so few at the most, as com-
pared with the eternal ages—in things that are of
no lasting profit.

Paul was an example both in life and doctrine
for all who should come after him. It was not a
prideful egotism that led him to plead with saints
to follow him and his faithful companions as they
followed Christ. He *lived* what he taught. His
life was the practical exemplification of his teaching. He was not one man on the platform or in
the meeting, and another in private or in business
life. For we need to remember that Paul was no
gentleman of leisure. He was not a clergyman
afraid to soil his hands with honest labor. He
wrought night and day tent-making, when funds
were low or when he felt the need of setting an
example of activity to any inclined to slothfulness; yet all the while preaching and teaching
publicly and from house to house with a diligence
that few if any have equalled, and none have sur-
passed. He was careful also as to his personal
communion with the Lord, striving to keep a
conscience ever void of offence toward both God
and man. What an example for us all to
follow!

That he could not please everybody, even his
own brethren, at all times, goes without saying.

His work was belittled, his appearance ridiculed, his apostleship denied, and his integrity called in question. There were those who even intimated that he was a crafty deceiver who, by an appearance of frankness, caught with guile the unwary, and at times did evil that good might come! All these charges and insinuations he indignantly refutes in various parts of his writings, while never allowing calumnies to embitter him. He did not return railing for railing, or seek to injure those who would so willingly have injured him. He kept on the even tenor of his way, *living* Christ and *preaching* Christ with unchanged ardor to the very end; his wondrous life stood as an abiding answer to those who would malign him. Therefore he could say, "Be followers together of me," and he could consistently call upon the saints to mark his ways and to walk in the same paths.

And though centuries have rolled by since wicked men sought to dishonor him, and the executioner's axe severed his hoary head from his body by Cæsar's order, thus finishing his testimony in laying down his life for his Master's sake, he still remains the pre-eminent example of what the Christian should be, sustained by grace divine while passing through this valley of death's shadow. Let us examine our own ways and see how

they measure up to his—not excusing ourselves
for failure on the score that times and conditions
have changed from those that surrounded him.
The same One who wrought effectually in him so
long ago, will work in us to-day if there be but
a willing mind and a sanctified determination to
take his path of unworldliness and devotion to
Christ.

Of an altogether different class the next two
verses warn us. Many there were, then as now,
who, while professing to be in the pilgrim path,
walked in a vain show; by word proclaiming
themselves Christians, but by their actions prov-
ing that they were enemies of the cross of Christ.
Mark it well: they were not said to be enemies of
the *blood* or of the *death* of Christ; their opposition was directed against that which told of His
shame and rejection by the world—*His cross*. In
that cross Paul gloried. By it he saw himself
crucified unto the world and the world unto him.
But the world-lovers refused this. They desired
the benefits of His death while refusing to be
identified with His *shame*. They lived for self-
indulgence, yet made a pretence of piety. The expression, "Whose God is their belly," really means
that they worshiped themselves. "Belly" is self-
gratification; and, alas, how many live for self!
And yet it is out of this same self, or person, that,

when devoted to Christ, living waters shall flow for the refreshment and blessing of others, as our Lord says in the seventh of John. Until self is thus displaced as an object for which to live, and surrendered to God as an instrument to be used by and for Christ, there can be no true pilgrim character.

The apostle declares that for these enemies of the cross the end will be destruction. Consider for a moment the solemnity of this. They lived for self-gratification while in this scene; in the life to come they will be in a condition where the gratification of the smallest desire will be utterly impossible. Our Lord told of one who on earth was clothed in purple and fine linen, and fared sumptuously every day, but when suddenly snatched away from it all by the rude hand of death, he found himself in greatest torment, where not even his anguished prayer for a drop of water to cool his parched tongue could be granted. Such is the destruction awaiting those who live for self, ignoring the claims of the Christ of God. And yet, heedless of all this, they go on in their folly, indifferent alike to the admonitions of Scripture, of conscience, and of the Holy Spirit—indifferent also to the warnings and entreaties of men of God who, like Paul, have chosen the better part, and know whereof they speak.

Casting to the winds all godly counsel and sound
advice, like flamboyant fools sporting on the edge
of a moral precipice, displaying their heedlessness
and folly before all, they glory in their shame,
and exult in that which might well cause them to
bow in penitent grief before redeeming mercy.
Unlike Mary, who chose that good part never to
be taken from her; or like Moses, who chose to
suffer affliction with the people of God rather
than enjoy the pleasures of sin for a season, they
deliberately reject the good and choose the evil.
They put away the hope of heaven for a brief
season of sensual or sensuous pleasure here on
earth. It is all summed up in the four little words
— "Who mind earthly things." Despising the
heavenly calling, they choose the earthly, and become indeed "dwellers upon the earth," only to
be exposed to the fierce vials of the wrath of God
in the day when He arises to shake terribly the
earth. No wonder the apostle wept as he wrote
of such, and warned them of their peril in pur-
suing their evil ways.

Heavenly Citizenship

(chap. 3: 20, 21.)

"For our conversation (or, citizenship) is in heaven; from whence also we look for the (or, a) Saviour, the Lord Jesus Christ: who shall change our vile body (or, this body of our humiliation) that it may be fashioned like unto his glorious body (or, the body of his glory) according to the working whereby He is able even to subdue all things unto Himself."

THE Greek word *politeuma* here rendered "conversation" means, as is now well-known, commonwealth, citizenship, or it might almost be transliterated "politics," for it involves all three thoughts. The apprehension of its scope, as here used by the apostle, should help the Christian to understand his true relationship and position regarding the affairs of this life and of the earth.

Philippi was, when Paul wrote, a Roman colony. That is, as a mark of special favor, Roman citizenship had been granted to all the free-born citizens of the former Macedonian capital. This was considered a great privilege. It enabled each Philippian, though dwelling in Macedonia, to say proudly, "My citizenship is in Rome." His responsibilities were directly to the Imperial Power. He had to do with the Emperor, not with the

provincial government of Macedonia. Now, apply
this to the Christian. Saved by matchless grace,
though still living in the world, his commonwealth—the government to which he primarily
owes allegiance — is in heaven. He is directly
subject to the Lord Jesus Christ, and his conduct
is to be regulated by His Word. The realization
of this, while keeping him free from entangling
alliances with the affairs of this world, will not,
of course, tend to lawlessness or insubjection to
world-rulers. A Philippian, subject to imperial
authority, would not be a law-breaker in Macedonia, inasmuch as the same authority to which
he owed allegiance had instituted the government
of the country in which Philippi was the chief
city. And so the apostle tells us elsewhere, "The
powers that be are ordained of God," and he commands Christians to be subject in all things to
magistrates, as recognizing the divine authority
by which they rule.

But one will search in vain the distinctly Christian part of the Bible—namely, the New Testament Epistles—for any hint that Christians were
to seek worldly power or dominion during this
present age. Their place is that of subjection,
not rule, until Christ Himself returns to reign.

The Emperor, to whom the Philippians owed
allegiance, dwelt in Rome. Should he appear in

Philippi, he would recognize with special honor those whose citizenship was directly linked with the capital of the empire. *Our* Lord is in heaven, and from there we look to see Him soon descend, when He shall openly confess all those whose citizenship is in heaven—confess them before an astonished and affrighted world. (See 2 Thess. 1 : 3-12.)

It is now known, as a result of recent archeological discoveries, that the term *kurios* (the general word for "Lord" in the New Testament) was an imperial title. More than that, this imperial title was never used in reference to the emperors until, through a public ceremony, they were deified, according to pagan conceptions; therefore it was used as a divine title. At the very time that Paul wrote this letter, it was common to address the brutal man who occupied the imperial throne as "our Lord Nero," using the distinctive term just referred to. How marked the contrast, when the Christians, often writhing beneath the bitter persecutions of this unspeakably wicked tyrant, looked expectantly toward the heavens for the return of "our Lord Jesus Christ."

At His coming, the first resurrection will take place; the sleeping saints will be raised, and living saints will be changed. For "this corruptible must put on incorruption, and this mortal must

put on immortality" (1 Cor. 15 : 53), and our natural bodies will be changed to spiritual bodies.

It should be remembered that when our Bible
was translated in the 17th century, the word
"vile" did not necessarily have the thought of evil
connected with it. That was "vile" which was
lowly or common : so here "our vile body" is really
"the body of our humiliation"—the body which
links us with the lower creation ; a body common
to both saint and sinner. At the Lord's return it
will be transformed, and made like unto the body
of His glory. In that resurrection-body He came
forth from the tomb, was manifested to His disciples, ascended into heaven, appeared to Saul of
Tarsus, and in it He shall soon return with glory.
The natural body is really a *soulish* body, or soul-
ual, if we may coin the word ; and a spiritual body
is a body suited to the spirit. It is not that one
is material and the other immaterial : for both
are material, though the one is of finer substance
than "this mortal body," and no longer subject
to certain laws by which the natural body is now
controlled. In *bodies* of glory, then, we shall
dwell forever in the city to which we even now
belong. It is our own, our native country, as
children of God ; and we shall never really be at
home until we are there with our glorified Lord
Himself.

The same divine energy that wrought in Him to raise Him from the dead, shall still work through Him until He subdues all things to Himself. Then as we learn from 1 Cor. 15:24-28, He will deliver the kingdom to the Father, that God, in all His fulness—Father, Son, and Holy Spirit—may be all in all forever, and fully manifested in Christ Jesus, who remains eternally our Lord and our Head.

CHAPTER FOUR

*CHRIST, THE BELIEVER'S STRENGTH, AND THE
CONFIDENT MIND*

Exhortation to Unity

(vers. 1-3.)

"Therefore, my brethren dearly beloved and longed for,
my joy and crown, so stand fast in the Lord, my dearly beloved. I beseech Euodia, and beseech Syntyche, that they
be of the same mind in the Lord. And I entreat thee also,
true yokefellow, help those women which labored with me
in the gospel, with Clement also, and with other my fellow-
laborers, whose names are in the book of life."

THE long parenthesis of the third chapter
concluded, the apostle again exhorts to
steadfastness and unity. It is very evident that there was incipient division of some
nature working in the Philippian assembly. It
was in order to meet this, as we have already noticed, that the letter was written; but Paul did
not immediately put his finger upon the difficulty.
Through the three previous chapters he has been
ministering that which should prepare the hearts
of the offenders for a final word of exhortation.
In this section, he calls them by name, and pleads
with them not to let self-interest hinder the work
of the Lord.

With expressions of deepest affection, he addresses the assembly as a whole. They are his brethren, dearly beloved, for whom he yearns, and who will be, at the judgment-seat of Christ, his joy and crown. It will be noticed that this expression is analogous to that of 1 Thess. 2: 19, 20. There, addressing the saints who had been won to Christ through his ministry, he could say, "For what is our hope, or joy, or crown of rejoicing? Are not even ye in the presence of our Lord Jesus Christ at his coming? For ye are our glory and joy." When, as a servant, he stands at the judgment-seat of Christ, that which will fill his heart with gladness will be the sight of those for whose eternal blessing he had been used while laboring in this scene. Rutherford beautifully expresses the same thought when, speaking of the town in which he had labored so long, he cries,

"Oh, if one soul from Anwoth
Meet me at God's right hand,
My heaven will be two heavens,
In Immanuel's land."

Then he that soweth and he that reapeth will rejoice together, as each servant shall come bringing in his sheaves, and, looking up into the face of the Lord, will be able to say, "Behold I and the children whom God hath given me."

The crown of rejoicing is the soul-winner's garland, composed of those he has won for Christ. Such must ever stand in a more precious relationship to the one who has been used to their conversion than they possibly can to any other. They are his children in the faith; his sons and daughters in Christ Jesus. Their happy progress in the things of God gladdens his heart, and is, in itself, rich reward for his service in their behalf; while, on the other hand, their failure or break-down by the way, as evidenced by loss of interest in divine things, dissension, worldly ways again taken up, must rend his heart with grief, and also fill him with a certain sense of shame. "Now we live," writes the apostle elsewhere, "if ye stand fast in the Lord." A brother-servant, the apostle John, writing to his converts, says, "And now, little children, abide in Him; that, when He shall appear, we may have confidence, and not be ashamed before Him at his coming" (1 John 2:28). Notice, it is not that *they* may not be ashamed, but "we," that is, those who were instrumental in leading them to Christ.

So it is in view of all this that Paul earnestly exhorts his beloved Philippians to stand fast in the faith. It is always the effort of Satan to hinder the people of God from steadfastly clinging together, and presenting a united front to the enemy. Alas, that his efforts to introduce dissension so readily succeed because of the flesh in us.

And now, without further delay, and in perfect frankness, the apostle speaks directly to the two offenders against unity, whom he had in his mind from the beginning. And yet there is no sternness, no seeking to lord it over their consciences, but he pleads with them, as though Christ Himself were beseeching, and entreats Euodia and Syntyche. They had been earnest laborers in the gospel, but had fallen out with each other, as we say, and they are exhorted to be of the same mind in the Lord. He certainly does not mean by this that they must think alike in everything, or see all things from the same standpoint. This can never be while we are in this world. The very possession of mind, which differentiates man from the brutes, of necessity gives occasion for differences of judgment as to many things, and so calls for much patience toward one another. No two men ever saw the same rainbow. The slightest difference of position gives each a view at a different angle. The formation and contour of the eye itself has to be taken in consideration. One may discern clearly every distinct shade, while the other may be color-blind, and no amount of argument or persuasion will enable the second to see that which is so clear to the first. And so

we may even say no two men have ever read the
same Bible. Not that there is one book from God
for one person and a different one for another,
but the difference is in our apprehension of
things. We are so influenced by our environment,
by our education, or lack of it, that we are pre-
judiced when we least realize it; and, even when
we try to be the most open-minded, we are often
misled by our impressions and the limitations of
our understanding. Therefore, the need of great
patience one with the other.

But if what we have been saying is true, how
then can we be of one mind? The verse does not
end without making that very plain: "I beseech
Euodia, and beseech Syntyche," he writes, "that
they be of the same mind *in the Lord*." If both
alike have the mind of Christ—which is the lowly
mind—if both alike seek to be subject to the Lord,
even though there may be differences of judgment
as to many things, each will respect the other's
view-point, and neither will try to force the other's
conscience. Thus all occasion for dissension would
be at an end. Alas, that we so little realize this,
and are often so insistent on what seems to us
exceedingly important truth, when nothing vital
is at stake, while a brother or sister equally honest
and earnest may fail to see things as we see
them; and, at the judgment-seat of Christ, it may

be manifested that, after all, they, and not we, were right, or perhaps that both were wrong.

I take it that the third verse was spoken by Paul to Epaphroditus personally, who was, I presume, his amanuensis in the writing of this letter. He was about to return to Philippi, having fulfilled his mission, and now, strengthened after his illness, was to be the bearer of this epistle. The apostle entreats him, as a true yokefellow, to help these women upon his return, to that unity of mind to which he had been exhorting them. He mentions that they had labored with him in the gospel, with Clement also, and with others of his fellow-laborers, whose names though not given here, are in the book of life. We are not to understand by this that they occupied the public platform or taught in the assembly of God, participating, with Paul and Clement and these other laborers, in public testimony: for this would contradict the words of the Holy Ghost through the same apostle, as preserved for us in 1 Cor. 14 and in 1 Tim. 2; but there were many ways in which devoted women could serve the Lord in the gospel. In fact, in oriental, as well as in occidental lands, work for women is of tremendous importance. There were many places where a man could not go, where godly women may have free access. And "laboring in the gospel" implies a great deal more than simply speaking from a platform. In fact, it is a question if this latter be not, in many instances at least, the lesser thing, and the individual heart-to-heart work the greater.

It seems clear that Epaphroditus caught the note of inspiration in these personal words to him, and so he embodied them in this letter; and we can be thankful to God that they have come down to us, for they give us deeper insight into the working of the spirit of grace in the mind of Paul, and will be valuable to all who seek to serve the Lord, until the Church's history on earth is ended.

Joy and Peace
(chap. 4: 4-7.)

"Rejoice in the Lord always: and again I say, Rejoice. Let your moderation be known unto all men. The Lord is at hand. Be careful for nothing: but in every thing by prayer and supplication with thanksgiving let your requests be made known unto God: and the peace of God, which passeth all understanding, shall keep your hearts and minds through Christ Jesus."

IN the opening verse of chapter 3 we have already had the exhortation, "Finally, my brethren, rejoice in the Lord." Undoubtedly, the apostle was, so far as his own mind was concerned, just ready to bring his letter to a close. But, as we have already seen, this was not the mind of the Spirit, and, like his brother-apostle, Jude, on another occasion, he was "borne along" to exhort the saints to "earnestly contend for the faith once delivered." Now he again refers to that which was so much upon his heart. He would have the saints always rejoicing in the Lord. Joy and holiness are inseparable. A holy Christian is able to rejoice even when passing through deepest afflictions; but a believer who, through unwatchfulness, has permitted himself to fall into unholy ways, loses immediately the joy of the Lord, which is the strength of those who walk in communion with Himself.

The second exhortation is one to which we may well give earnest heed. In the Authorized Version we read, "Let your moderation be known unto all men." Undoubtedly, "moderation" is a most commendable Christian virtue, but there is more to the original word than this. It has been rendered by some "yieldingness;" this, too, is an excellent translation, so far as it goes, and suggests that resilience of character which many of us sadly lack. Rotherham gives "considerateness," which adds to the thought, and helps us to a better understanding of the mind of the Spirit in this connection. The Revised Version has "forbearance," and "gentleness" in the margin. But if we take all these various terms we shall, I think, find them

summed up in the very suggestive rendering given
years ago by Matthew Arnold, the English critic,
who translated the passage, "Let your *sweet rea-
sonableness* be manifested to all men." He pointed out the interesting fact that the word here
used is unknown in classical Greek and it was
his impression that Paul coined it for the occasion. What a lovely trait is this sweet reasonable-
ness in a Christian! It is the very opposite to
that unyielding, harshly-dogmatic, self-determined
spirit, that so often dominates in place of the
meekness and gentleness of Christ. "I beseech
you, my brethren," wrote Cromwell to the war-
ring theologians of his day, "remember that it is
possible you *may* be wrong." How apt we are to
forget this when engaged in discussions as to
either doctrines, methods of service, or church
principles!

This does not mean that one need be lacking in
intensity of conviction or assurance as to the cor-
rectness of doctrines, principles or practices
which one believes he has learned from the word
of God; but it does imply a kindly consideration
for the judgment of others, who may be equally
sincere, and equally devoted—and, possibly, even
more enlightened. Nothing is ever lost by recognizing this, and remembering that we all know
in part.

How aptly the brief sentence, "The Lord is at hand" comes in, in connection with the preceding exhortation! I take it that the thought is not exactly "The Lord is coming;" it is rather, "The Lord is standing by;" He is looking on; He hears every word spoken; He takes note of every action.

> "Closer is He than breathing,
> Nearer than hands or feet."

With the realization that He is thus, in the fullest sense, "at hand," though unseen, how quickly would strife and dissension cease, and the forbearance and grace ever manifested in Himself be seen in His followers!

And now we have a wonderful promise based on a third exhortation; this time in connection with prayer. Our Lord Himself has warned against anxious thought, and the Holy Spirit expands His teaching by saying, "In nothing be anxious." But how am I to obey an exhortation like this when troubles are surging around me, and my poor, restless mind will not be at peace? I feel I must tell somebody. My exercises are like those of the Psalmist perhaps, who wrote on one occasion, "I am so agitated that I cannot speak" (Ps. 77: 4, *F. W. Grant's Trans.*). What, then shall I do? To whom shall I turn? It is so natural to worry and fret under circumstances such as these; though I tell myself over and over again that nothing is gained thereby, and my trouble only seems to become exaggerated as I try to carry my own burdens.

But the Spirit of God points the way out. He would have me bring everything, the great things and the little things, perplexing conditions and trying circumstances of every character, into the presence of God, and *leave them there*. By prayer and supplication, not forgetting thanksgiving for past and present mercies, He would have me pour out my requests unto God. I may feel that I do not know the mind of the Lord in regard to them, but that need not hinder. I am to make known my "requests," counting on His wisdom to do for me that which is best both for time and eternity. Thus, casting my care upon Him, and leaving all in His own blessed hands, the peace of God (that peace which He, Himself, ever enjoys, though storms and darkness may be round about), a peace passing all understanding, shall guard, as with a military garrison, my heart: and (blessed truth, if I but enter into it) my *thoughts,* or "mind," as it is here translated, through Christ Jesus.

But this I cannot do for myself. I may tell myself over and over that I will not worry, will not fret, but my thoughts, like untamed horses with the bit in their teeth, if I may use such an illustration, seem to run away with me. Or, like an attacking army, they crowd into the citadel of my mind, and threaten to overwhelm me. But God, Himself, by the Holy Spirit, has engaged to so garrison my mind, and so protect my restless heart, that my thoughts shall neither run away with me, nor yet overwhelm me. Every thought will be brought into captivity to the obedience of Christ. Thus I shall enjoy the peace of God, a peace beyond all human comprehension, as I leave my burdens where faith delights to cast every care, at the feet of Him who, having not withheld His own Son, has now declared that through Him He will freely give me all things. In this I can rest, for He cannot deny Himself.

Exhortations

(chap. 4: 8, 9.)

"Finally, brethren, whatsoever things are true, whatsoever things are honest, whatsoever things are just, whatsoever things are pure, whatsoever things are lovely, whatsoever things are of good report; if there be any virtue, and if there be any praise, think on these things. Those things, which ye have both learned, and received, and heard, and seen in me, do; and the God of peace shall be with you."

THESE verses conclude the instructions of the apostle; all that follows being in the nature of a postscript—and, while of deep practical value, not directly addressed to saints as homiletical teaching.

Having throughout the epistle put Christ before his readers in so many different aspects, the apostle now sums all up in this brief exhortation to think on things holy, thus recognizing the Old Testament principle, "As a man thinketh in his heart, so is he." Many have missed the very point, however, which it seems clear he is pressing, by taking all these things in an abstract way. It will be found exceedingly difficult to think on things true, honest, just, pure, and lovely, if there be not some definite, concrete example before the mind. Mere occupation with beautiful sentiments and poetic ideals is not, I take it, what he would here inculcate. But all are found fully exemplified in our Lord Jesus Christ as the perfect Man here on earth; and, in measure, these qualities are reproduced by the Holy Spirit in all who have been made partakers of the divine nature. In a certain sense we may think of these words as linking with the exhortation already given to Euodia and Syntyche, who needed to see in each other what the Spirit had wrought.

Let Euodia look coldly and critically upon Syntyche, and occupy her mind with whatever she can find in her character or ways that is contrary to the virtues here mentioned, and the breach between them will be immeasurably widened. Let Syntyche retort by exaggerating every defect or short-coming in her sister in Christ, and she will soon become so alienated from her that reconciliation will be almost impossible.

But, on the other hand, if Euodia, realizing that Syntyche has been redeemed to God by the same precious blood as herself, and is indwelt by the same Holy Spirit, determines to think of the virtues or anything worthy of praise in her life and personality; to magnify her graces and minimize her faults, refusing to indulge in unkind criticism, she will be so attracted by what is of Christ in her that she will find herself linked in heart to the one from whom she had previously turned coldly away.

Is not this what we all greatly need in our dealings with each other? In every truly converted soul there are the manifest inwrought virtues of the Spirit of God ; things that are honest, just, pure, lovely and of good report—the activities of the new nature. If we think on these things, instead of dwelling upon the failures to which all are liable, our fellowship one with another will become increasingly precious as the days go by. And even when there is actual cause for blame, if we stop to consider the circumstances that may

have led up to that which seems to us so blame-
worthy, Christian pity and compassion will take
the place of criticism and unkind judgment, which
cannot help to restore, but only serves to drive
farther into sin the erring one. "To err is human; to forgive divine." And even a poet of this
world has taught us the folly of judging that
which the eye cannot see, when, in his quaint
Scottish way, he has written,

> "We only ken the wrang that's dune,
> We ken na' what's resisted."

We may severely blame the wrong-doer for
things that have already deeply exercised his
heart and conscience, and been long since cleansed
away by the washing of water by the Word as ap-
plied by the Lord Jesus Himself.

And, of course, in all our ways it is important
that we should never permit our minds to feed,
like carrion vultures, on the wicked, filthy, and
unholy things of the flesh. This is thoroughly
natural to the carnal man, and the carnal mind
is still in the believer, and will be until the day
when our bodies of humiliation shall be changed
and made like His body of glory. But we are not
to permit it to dominate us, since the Holy Spirit
dwells in us to control us for Christ. There is so
much that is honest; so much that is just or right-

eous; so much that is pure; so much that is lovely
and loveable; so much that is of good report; so
much that is virtuous and trustworthy, that it
were folly to be occupied with the opposites, when
we might be taken up with positive good.

And, as we meditate on these things, we grow
in grace and in the knowledge of our Lord Jesus
Christ; for, as we have already noted, all these
beautiful traits were fully exemplified in Him,
and they have been imparted, in large measure, to
each of His servants; probably to none more so
than the writer of this epistle. Therefore, without pride, but as an example to the flock of Christ,
he can add, "Those things, which ye have both
learned, and received, and heard, and seen in me,
do." And as thus practically walking, according
to the power of the indwelling Spirit, we have the
sweet assurance that "the God of peace shall be
with you," thus connecting all this with the promise of verse 7 above, where we are assured that
"the peace of God" shall garrison the minds and
hearts of all who cast their every care on Him.
Here we learn that the God of peace will walk
with those who seek to walk before Him in piety
and holiness of mind and ways.

Ministry in Temporal Things

(chap. 4: 10-23.)

"But I rejoiced in the Lord greatly, that now at the last your care of me hath flourished again; wherein ye were also careful, but ye lacked opportunity. Not that I speak in respect of want: for I have learned, in whatsoever state I am, therewith to be content. I know both how to be abased, and I know how to abound: everywhere and in all things I am instructed both to be full and to be hungry, both to abound and to suffer need. I can do all things through Christ which strengtheneth me. Notwithstanding ye have well done, that ye did communicate with my affliction. Now ye Philippians know also, that in the beginning of the gospel, when I departed from Macedonia, no church communicated with me as concerning giving and receiving, but ye only. For even in Thessalonica ye sent once and again unto my necessity. Not because I desire a gift: but I desire fruit that may abound to your account. But I have all, and abound: I am full, having received of Epaphroditus the things which were sent from you, an odour of a sweet smell, a sacrifice acceptable, well-pleasing to God. But my God shall supply all your need according to his riches in glory by Christ Jesus. Now unto God and our Father be glory for ever and ever. Amen. Salute every saint in Christ Jesus. The brethren which are with me greet you. All the saints salute you, chiefly they that are of Cæsar's household. The grace of our Lord Jesus Christ be with you all. Amen."

IN this, the closing section of the epistle, Paul thanks the assembly at Philippi for the practical way in which they had manifested their fellowship in the gospel. They were not of those who are willing to profit eternally through the gospel ministry, but have very little exercise as to the temporal welfare of the servants of Christ to whom they owe the knowledge of that truth which has made them free. From the beginning of their Christian lives, the Philippian saints had cared, as occasion offered, for the needs of the apostle, even sending to him of their substance when he was laboring in Thessalonica, where he and his companions had gone after being released from the Philippian jail. But years had elapsed since then, and Paul had travelled far, and passed through many varied experiences, often finding it quite impossible to keep in close touch with the different assemblies he had been used of God to establish. Consequently it was not strange that, at times, it should seem as if his dearest friends had forgotten him. Nevertheless, the love was there though they had lacked opportunity to display it. But now they had learned of his circumstances, as a prisoner in Rome for the truth's sake, and they had hastened to show their fellowship with him in his sufferings, by sending Epaphroditus with a gift of love, as we have already noticed.

In acknowledging this, Paul takes occasion to glorify God for His care of him, even when Christian assemblies forgot their indebtedness to him. He had indeed known cold neglect and indifference, but it never soured his spirit nor led him to complain. He noted the cold-heartedness, but he did not find fault. He left it all with the Lord, and committed his own circumstances to Him, assured that *He* never forgot, and was never an unconcerned spectator of His servant's sufferings. So, he accepted it all as a course in the school of God, and he could say, "I have learned in whatsoever state I am to be content." The Lord was his portion, and he could rest in the knowledge of His unchanging love and care.

It was not in a moment that he entered into this. He, like all disciples in God's school, had to advance in the life of faith by learning practically the things he could now teach to others. But he had taken his degree, so to speak, and he could now declare, "I know both how to be abased, and to abound; everywhere, and in all things, I possess the secret (or, I have been initiated) both to be full, and to be hungry, to abound and to suffer need." Blessed lessons these! And we may say the soul is never really at rest in regard to the trials and testings of the way until these precious secrets have been apprehended.

John Wesley is reported to have said that he did not know which dishonored God the most—to worry, which is really to doubt His love and care, or to curse and swear. Yet every saint would shrink from the latter with abhorrence, while many of us have no sense of the wrong we do when we fret and worry. To rest in faith upon the knowledge that "all things work together for good to those who love God, who are the called according to His purpose," should ever be our attitude. And in a very special sense they who minister in word and doctrine (in entire dependence on the One who has sent them out as His ambassadors) are called upon to exemplify this in their calm dependence upon Him whom they serve.

This leads me to say something upon the New Testament principle for the support of those who labor entirely in spiritual things. And, first, let it be noted carefully, there is no such thing known in Scripture as putting the servant of God upon the low level of a salary basis. The only man mentioned in the Bible to be hired by the year as a "minister" was the recreant Levite who was engaged by Micah of Mount Ephraim, and later by the Danites to be their "father and priest" (Judges, chaps. 17 and 18). Even in the legal dispensation, Jehovah Himself was the portion of the Levites. They were prospered, and cared for, in accordance with the measure in which God blessed

His people and their hearts responded to His goodness. In the Christian economy we have no special clerical or extra-priestly class to be supported as professional men by their so-called laybrethren. The distinction of clergy and laity is utterly unscriptural, and is but part of the Judaizing system that has so perverted the truth of the Church. But there are those who are specially gifted as evangelists, pastors, and teachers, and who, in many instances, though not in all, are called upon to separate themselves from secular pursuits in order to give their time unhinderedly to spiritual service. These of old "went forth for the Name's sake," we are told in 3rd John, "taking nothing of the Gentiles." They were cast entirely on the Lord, and He cared for them through His own grateful people, according to the word, "Let him that is taught in the Word communicate unto him that teacheth in all good things." And so John, by the Spirit, writes, "We therefore ought to receive such that we might be fellow-helpers to the truth." Such servants have a claim upon the people of God, not because they are official ministers, but because they are engaged in making known the truth, and in this service all believers are privileged to share.

But observe carefully :—the servant is never to look to the saints for his support, but to count directly on the Lord, and make his personal needs known only to Him. He need not fear to acquaint the assemblies with special opportunities for ministry to others as occasions arise. Paul did this frequently and earnestly. But rather than mention his personal needs, he would labor with his own hands; nor did he feel he was degrading his calling in so doing—that thus he might provide things honest in the sight of all men, and set an example to any who might be inclined to seek an easy path, and depend upon support by those in better circumstances than themselves.

And so the principle is clear: the servant of Christ is to go forth in absolute dependence upon the One who has commissioned him, and who makes Himself responsible to meet his needs. But the people of God are called upon to be exercised before Him as to what share they should have in the support of those who are thus engaged. No ministering brother has the right or authority to demand support from the saints. They, not he, must judge whether he is worthy of that support. But, on the other hand, if receiving from him in spiritual things, it is, we are told, a small matter that he should reap their carnal things. "They that preach the gospel should live of the gospel" (1 Cor. 9).

For a servant of the Lord to be finding fault be-

cause of the smallness of his support, is to make
manifest at once that his dependence is upon man
rather than on God; and for saints to be callously
indifferent to the temporal needs of those whom
they recognize as God-sent messengers, is to show
themselves out of touch with Him who has given
to them the privilege of being in this way fellow-
helpers to the truth. Thus should both those who
minister and those who are ministered to, be exercised before God as to their mutual responsibilities.

This had been the path in which Paul had
walked for many years, and as he looked back
over the journey and saw how he had been sustained of God, he knew he could count on Him
for the future, and so he faced the days to come
with the assurance that he could do all things
through Christ who was his strength. He who
was to him life, example, and object, was also his
unfailing source of supply for every emergency
that might arise, even to a martyr's death.

But while he did not look to man for his sup-
plies, he shows himself truly grateful for the
ministry extended to him. He would not take the
gift of love sent by his dear Philippian children
in the faith as though it were a mere matter of
course. He expresses himself in most apprecia-
tive terms as he thanks them for their fellowship,

and in this he is an example to all Christ's servants, some of whom have been only too neglect-
ful of the finer courtesies which often mean more
to the saints than they realize.

Paul received the gift not because he desired to
profit by means of their generosity, but because
he saw in it an added evidence of the working of
the Spirit of grace in their souls, and this was for
their blessing, as well as relieving his need. And
so he gladly accepted it all, seeing in it "an odor
of a sweet savor, a sacrifice acceptable and well-
pleasing to God."

Nor would He, for whose glory they ministered
the gift to His imprisoned servant, allow them to
put Him in their debt, but engaged Himself to
supply all their need, according to *His* riches in
glory, through Christ Jesus. The more blessed
part must always be His, for when we have given
to our utmost limit, we have only returned Him a
little of His own, and even that He will abun-
dantly repay.

The last three verses give the concluding salutation. Note again how "every saint" is affec-
tionately greeted. He would refuse to the last to
recognize any parties among them. And all with
him joined in saluting them—particularly some,
evidently newly come to the faith, and possibly as

a result of coming in contact with him in his prison-cell, whom he mentions as "those of Cæsar's household," who belonged to the imperial guard.

And so we close our meditations on this instructive epistle with a message of "grace" ringing in our souls.   H. A. I.

The Complete Writings of H. A. Ironside

By H. A. IRONSIDE

GOSPEL TRACTS

Add 10% for postage to all orders less than $2.50